DR. JACK VAN IMPE

Dynamic and Dedicated

A Man and His Mission

© 2006 by Jack Van Impe Ministries
All rights reserved

Some text excerpted from *They Call Him The Walking Bible* by Roger F. Campbell, © 1977 by Jack Van Impe Crusades, and from *Perhaps Today* Magazine, published by Jack Van Impe Ministries—January/February 1985, May/June 1988, and July/August 1988 issues.

Photographs from Jack Van Impe Ministries archives, with the following exceptions:
Photos pp. Cover, inside cover, 1, 2-3, 4, 24, 58, 66, 84, 88, 98, 102, 134, 138, 147, 150 – Adobe® Stock Photos
Photo pp. 116-117 © Marc Tauss/Photonica

JVIM Coordinating Editor: Dr. Rexella Van Impe
And with appreciation to the following for their participation in this project:
James H. Kerby, concept and copy; Dr. Charles (Chuck) Ohman, Vice President and television announcer.

Interior design by Carol L. Restovic

All Scripture quotations, unless otherwise indicated, are taken from the *Holy Bible,* King James Version.

ISBN 1-884137-56-3

Printed in U.S.A.

Contents

THE BEGINNING
1948 1

THE MINISTRY TODAY
Taking Christ's Love Into Every Man's World 4
Doing God's Work…God's Way 6
A Master Plan For Soulwinning 7

THE MAKING OF A MAN OF GOD
A Prophetic Voice For This Age—
Preparing The Way For Christ's Return 12
I Must Be About My Father's Business 14
The Walking Bible 16
Driven By An All–Consuming Passion 20

THE TENDER TOUCH
Rexella Van Impe—Partner In Life And Ministry .. 24
Whither Thou Goest, I Will Go… 26

AMBASSADORS FOR CHRIST
What On Earth Are We Doing? 32
Doing The Work Of An Evangelist 37
Stir The Saints…Save The Sinners 42
Letters We Love…
…About The Local Church Crusades 48

TOOLS OF EVANGELISM
Records And Tapes 50
Letters We Love…
…About Records And Tapes 52

GO YE INTO ALL THE WORLD
Reaching The Mission Field 54
Letters We Love…
…From Around The World 56

AMERICA'S EVANGELIST TO THE WORLD
Using Radio To Take The Gospel To All Nations ... 58
Letters We Love…
…About Global Radio Outreach 60
Am Not I Better To Thee Than Ten Sons? 62

DR. JACK VAN IMPE, CHRISTIAN SCHOLAR
Study To Show Thyself Approved Unto God 64

A VOICE CRYING IN THE WILDERNESS OF OUR TIME
Prime Time Television 66
Letters We Love…
…About National Television Specials 70
A Flame of Hope, Light, and Power…
Proclaiming The Truth Of Christ's Revelation 72
Souls Unlimited 74
Earnestly, Tenderly, Jesus Is Calling,
"Oh, Sinner, Come Home!" 76
He Shall Give His Angels Charge Over Thee,
To Keep Thee In All Thy Ways 78
Letters We Love…
…About The Areawide Crusades 80

WALKING THROUGH THE VALLEY OF THE SHADOW
Any Attacker Would Have To
Go Through God's Hand To Get To Us 84

HEART DISEASE IN CHRIST'S BODY
Revival, Redemption, and Reconciliation 88
5,000 Christian Leaders Responded To
Jack Van Impe's Impassioned Call To Unity 92

Contents (continued)

HEART DISEASE IN CHRIST'S BODY (continued)
Letters We Love…
…Responses to *Heart Disease* Book 94
A More Sure Word Of Prophecy 96

FENICA: CHOSEN FRIENDS
"She Was A Stray And We Took Her In." 98

JACK VAN IMPE PRESENTS…
Reaching More People In One Night
Than In A Lifetime of Crusades 102
Owe No Man Anything! 104
Declare Ye Among The Nations,
Publish…And Conceal Not 108
Letters We Love…
…About Publications & Literature 110
Write Thee All The Words That
I Have Spoken Unto Thee In A Book 112
Letters We Love…
…About The Book Ministry 114
I Was In Prison And Ye Came To Me 116
Letters We Love…
…About The Prison Ministry 118

ENLARGE THE PLACE OF THY TENT
Jack Van Impe Ministries International
World Outreach Center 120
We Are Labourers Together With God 122

NEW TELEVISION FORMAT: JACK VAN IMPE PRESENTS
Interpreting Today's News
In The Light Of Bible Prophecy 124
Letters We Love…
…About The Weekly Telecast 130

VIDEO EVANGELISM
Sharing The Truth Of God's Word In
The Homes Of Spiritually Hungry People 134
Letters We Love…
About The Video Ministry 136

HTTP://WWW.JVIM.COM
Instant Access To Ministry Help From Anywhere
In The World…Via The Internet 138
Letters We Love…
…From Our Internet Site 140

OSCAR & LOUISE VAN IMPE
"For I Was My Father's Son, Tender And
Only Beloved In The Sight Of My Mother." 142

REX & ESTHER SHELTON
"Thy Father And Thy Mother Shall Be Glad,
And She That Bare Thee Shall Rejoice." 144

WHAT OTHERS SAY
Comments by Friends And Fellow Laborers 147

THERE IS NO STOPPING PLACE
What Happens To A Man Of God
After Fifty Years Of Ministry? 150

DR. JACK VAN IMPE

Dynamic and Dedicated

A Man and His Mission

In 1948
The eyes of the world were
focused upon the Middle East
as the Jewish people of Palestine
and the world proclaimed a
"declaration of Independence"
...and the modern state of Israel
was born.

Half a world away,
in America's city of Detroit,
a new Christian,
the son of Belgian immigrants,
entered Bible college that same year
and began a ministry that was
to make a dramatic impact for Christ
around the globe...

The Ministry Today

Taking Christ's Love Into Every Man's World

Today...

More than 58 years after first responding to the call of God to **Go ye into all the world, and preach the gospel to every creature (Mark 16:15).**

Dr. Jack Van Impe is the most listened-to prophetic voice in the world.

Harnessing the power of space-age communications tools to beam television and radio signals 22,300 miles into space to orbiting satellite transmitters, Jack and Rexella Van Impe literally speak from the roof of the world and "give the winds a mighty voice" that Jesus saves!

The ministry's *WEEKLY TELECAST,* "Jack Van Impe Presents..." is viewed from coast to coast in some 25,000 cities and towns in North America alone. Hundreds of TV stations and thousands of cable releases on multiple nationwide networks—including TBN, INSP, ACTS, VISION, WGN, and BET—carry the program. The telecast also reaches multiplied nations in Europe, all of the Caribbean, South Africa, and most of the world.

Using its own *SATELLITE UPLINK NETWORK,* the ministry's radio and television signals blanket entire continents with the gospel. Listeners from 160 nations—many of them in the prophetically sensitive areas of Eastern Europe and the Middle East—are responding to the message of God's love.

Although renowned and respected as a Bible scholar and prophecy expert, Dr. Jack Van Impe's central theme and message remains the basic, fundamental, simple truth that God so loved the world that he gave his only begotten Son, that whosoever believeth in him should not perish, but have everlasting life (John 3:16).

Jesus came to bring the message of love and hope to every man—the rich and the poor, the educated and the unlearned, the leaders of society and the outcasts of His day. He lived and died so that every person could experience the love and forgiveness of God.

Sharing that message with every man in his own neighborhood is the mission of this ministry. We must reach the lost wherever they are. We must go into every nation, state, city, village—into every home. We must go into the places where people live and work and play—to touch them at the point of their need.

The challenge grows bigger each day. The need is greater now than at any time in history. There are more still unreached, still lost, than ever before. So there is no stopping place, no justification for cutting back or slowing down. And that is why, after fifty years of continuous gospel ministry, Jack and Rexella Van Impe have no thoughts of retirement.

Today is simply a new opportunity to go with the gospel, to reach out in love, and to help carry out Christ's Great Commission.

Doing God's Work...God's Way

Nearly 2,000 years ago, God the Father sent His Son, Jesus, to personally re-establish the lines of communication—and fellowship—between God and man.

This fellowship had been interrupted by man's sinful disobedience in the Garden of Eden. Over the centuries, man had gotten farther and farther away from any meaningful understanding of God.

So Jesus came to earth… in the form of man. He was born in a stable, cradled in a manger, and grew up in a little country town in the home of a humble carpenter.

The Son of God did not dwell in a palace, or live as a prince, or set himself up as a king or ruler. He did not surround himself with luxury, or associate only with important people—with society's "upper crust."

Jesus set out to go into every man's world and show each person who God is and what He is really like. He went out to where men were plowing fields or mending fish nets by the sea. He went to village wells where women went to draw water. He had dinner in ordinary people's houses, attended weddings, visited local places of worship, and even spent time with those regarded as outcasts.

He fed the hungry, healed the sick, raised the dead. He brought help to the helpless, hope to the hopeless.

This humble man stood among the common people in His homespun robe, His dusty feet shod in plain leather sandals. But His words released a brilliant light into the darkened lives of the multitudes as He proclaimed, "If you want to know what God is like, look at Me. If you have seen Me, you have seen the Father" (see John 14:9).

Then He went to Golgotha and laid down His life on the cross to pay the penalty for sin… for all mankind. Once again man could come into the presence of God, unblemished and unafraid.

After defeating the power of death and hell through His resurrection, Jesus empowered His followers to be His witnesses in Jerusalem (their home town), in Judea (their nation), in Samaria (neighboring nations), and in all the known world (see Acts 1:8).

His commission was to go into all the world. His vision was for "every creature." His method was to touch and win "whosoever will," one by one.

This is the sole reason for the existence of Jack Van Impe Ministries. For 58 years Dr. Van Impe has been endeavoring to take the message of God's love into every man's world. It remains our enduring, unchanging purpose and goal for the future.

A Master Plan for Soulwinning

In fifty-eight years of evangelizing and soulwinning, Jack Van Impe Ministries has employed a variety of outreaches and methods to go into every man's world and present the love and hope found only in Christ. Each was developed and proven to be effective in reaching different groups of people with the gospel. In addition to the ministry's international television programming on broadcast stations and satellite networks, the following outreaches also have been or continue to be major soulwinning endeavors.

> *I am made all things to all men, that I might by all means save some. And this I do for gospel's sake.*
>
> —Paul the Apostle,
> 1 Corinthians 9:22,23

LOCAL CHURCH CRUSADES

As a teenager, before meeting and marrying Rexella, Jack was a frequent participant in Christian services for churches, youth rallies, and gospel groups of all kinds, both as an accomplished musician—"the nation's number one gospel accordionist"--and as a speaker. Throughout high school and Bible College, as he gained knowledge and experience, his zeal and dedication made him an effective and sought-after revival preacher.

Following their marriage, Jack and Rexella Van Impe crisscrossed America as "Ambassadors for Christ" in local church crusades. They conducted as many as 38 crusades a year, and were on the road up to 250 nights a year.

Revival broke out wherever they ministered, and they consistently broke attendance records. The Van Impe's sparkling music program attracted great crowds, and the impact of Jack's Bible-saturated messages filled the altars with converts and helped produce great spiritual renewal.

In the first two and a half decades, Jack Van Impe Ministries conducted some 800 local church crusades.

AREAWIDE CRUSADES

Reports of great crowds and unusual spiritual results in Van Impe crusades resulted in literally hundreds of invitations—more than they could have accepted in years of single church meetings! So the Van Impes began combining invitations from larger areas and conducting city- or area-wide crusades in large auditoriums and coliseums.

By enlisting the cooperative support of all Bible-believing, fundamentalist churches in an area, the Van Impes conducted some of the largest meetings in the history of American mass evangelism. They filled large civic auditoriums, coliseums, and sports stadiums across the nation. As one newspaper headline from this era noted: **200,000 Attend Crusades in 5 Weeks.**

Over a seventeen year period, the Jack Van Impe crusade team conducted more than 260 united areawide crusades, with ten million people in attendance. This is over and above the 800 local church crusades.

The Van Impe crusade outreach was among the most extensive efforts in mass evangelism of the twentieth century. It has been estimated that Dr. Jack Van Impe had preached the gospel, face to face, to more people than any other evangelist, except for the unparalleled record of Dr. Billy Graham.

PUBLICATIONS

In April 1979, the Van Impes launched their first regular printed contact with friends and supporters, an unassuming publication titled simply *Newsletter*. Through this vehicle, Jack kept people apprised of the Van Impe crusade itinerary, reported what was being accomplished in the meetings, and shared his observations and comments on the spiritual condition of America and the world.

Currently, the Van Impe's publish the bi-monthly magazine, *Perhaps Today,* which reaches 750,000 readers. Constantly looking forward to Christ's return, the 24-page, full-color magazine presents up-to-the-minute news headlines and their prophetic significance, along with scholarly articles by Dr. Van Impe, inspirational reflections by Rexella, a forum for letters from the ministry family, and much more.

RECORDINGS AND LITERATURE

Always an avid student of Bible prophecy, Jack prepared a message on "The Coming War With Russia" which created great interest wherever it was presented. Responding to the requests of people across the country, the message was put on a record and was an immediate best-seller! To date, more than 10,000 people have been converted through that one recording.

The Van Impes also produced several tremendously successful records of accordion music and vocal solos. They were presented a gold record in recognition of their producing and distributing a million recordings.

Now scores of Jack Van Impe messages are distributed on cassette tapes, including multi-tape prophetic teaching series. Several popular music cassettes by Rexella, "the first lady of sacred music," are also available.

The ministry also distributes literally tons of literature annually in the form of tracts and some 60 different booklets and books. Literature is sent across North America and into over 100 countries around the world, particularly in Asia and Africa.

GLOBAL RADIO

Today the Van Impe's gospel message is being broadcast to hungry hearts on every continent of the earth via Pan American Radio! People from 160 nations have responded to these Bible-centered, evangelistic messages of hope and love.

The Van Impe radio ministry was launched in 1971 with the simultaneous broadcast of the recorded sermon, "The Coming War With Russia," on 100 stations across the United States. The response from this single broadcast was so encouraging that a regular weekly program was begun the next year.

Again, the broadcast aired on a network of some 200 stations across the nation from the day of its inception. A year later, in January, 1973, the Van Impe radio program expanded its coverage to reach the world via the massive international coverage of Trans World Radio.

By 1977, the Jack Van Impe broadcast was being translated into 83 languages and aired on all the Trans World stations. TWR president, Dr. Paul E. Freed, acclaimed Dr. Jack Van Impe "America's first evangelist to the world!" He said the program translation project marked the first time in history any evangelist or religious organization had proclaimed the gospel to all the world in the languages of the people.

VIDEO PRESENTATIONS

One of the ministry's most effective outreaches is top-quality, high-impact audio tape and videotape productions for use in homes, churches, and Bible study groups. The Van Impes have released more than 150 major productions, with millions of copies in circulation.

Many of the videos were originally aired nation-wide as hour-long, prime-time television specials reaching millions of viewers. Audiences measured in millions viewed JVI productions such as *"The Occult World," "Russia, World War III* and *Armageddon," "Startling Revelations: Pope John Paul II," "2001: Countdown to Eternity," "The Spirit of Antichrist,"* and *"The Millennium."* Other productions include multiple-tape study series of Dr. Van Impe's major prophetic teachings, such as *"Revelation Revealed, Verse by Verse,"* and *"Daniel: Final End Time Mysteries Unsealed."*

The videos are powerful, portable evangelistic tools, which are viewed in the privacy of people's own homes, or shared with family, friends, and neighbors. Industry specialists have determined that as many as 20 people view the average video during its useful life. Using that criterion, the Van Impe video ministry alone has already touched the lives of some 25 million people.

PRISON MINISTRY

In response to the large number of prisoners being won to Christ through the Van Impe television programs who requested further assistance, the ministry set up a special outreach to serve them. Bibles, books, magazines, and selected Christian literature are distributed free of charge to inmates.

Working through prison chaplains, a specially designed in-depth Bible study course is being made available to serious, interested students. Hundreds of inmates each year in various penitentiaries across America and Canada are participating in this program.

The Van Impes also help support other established prison ministries that have effective outreaches to inmates. In addition, free literature is distributed through chaplains who minister in convalescent and nursing homes, hospitals, and rescue missions, as well as to men and women serving in various branches of the U.S. military services.

THE INTERNET

Continuing to use the most modern communications tools available, Jack Van Impe Ministries maintains an attractive "home page" on the World Wide Web. This information center is accessible to literally millions of people around the globe, 24 hours a day. Anyone with a computer and modem can access the ministry's Internet site at *http://www.jvim.com*.

Jack Van Impe Ministries' website features video and audio streaming of the weekly TV program, online editions of the monthly "Van Impe Intelligence Briefing" and bi-monthly *Perhaps Today* magazine, a daily news update section, weekly and daily devotionals, an extensive FAQ area on Bible prophecy, a new believers manual, a scripture memorization program, and full-text books by Van Impe. The site also includes the ministry's international TV schedule and a catalog section of ministry materials, including books, cassettes, and videos.

Recipient of the "Best of the Christian Web" award for 1997, the Van Impe cyberlink averages thousands of "hits" a day. Video streaming of the ministry's weekly telecast reaped 250,000 hits in its first month online—a tremendous new outreach for the gospel.

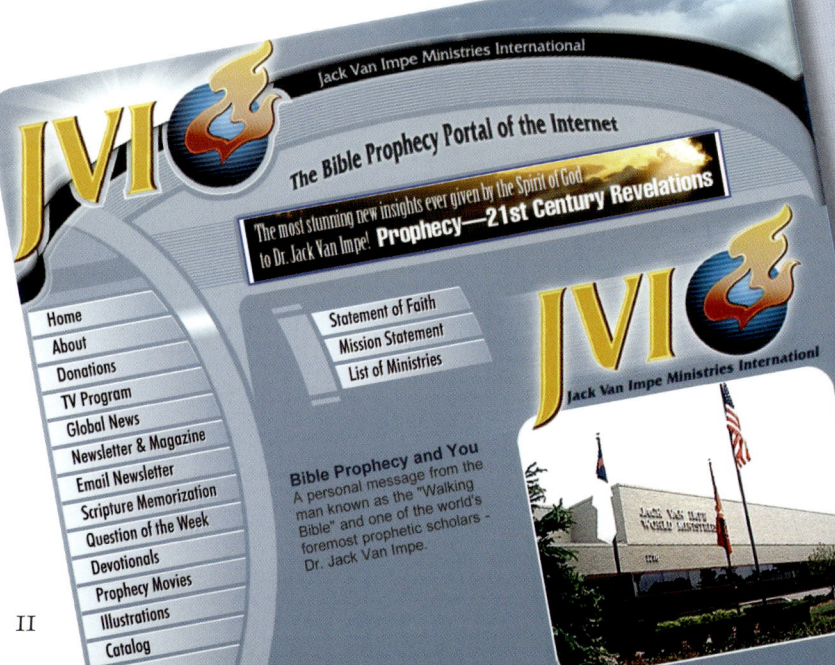

The Making of a Man of God

A Prophetic Voice for This Age

> And this gospel of the kingdom shall be preached in all the world for a witness unto all nations; and then shall the end come.
>
> —Matthew 24:14

Preparing The Way For Christ's Return

WHO IS DR. JACK VAN IMPE AND WHAT DOES HE STAND FOR?

He is a powerful gospel preacher. With his wife and ministry partner, Rexella, constantly at his side, Jack Van Impe has delivered the message of the gospel to live audiences totaling some ten million people.

He is an effective soulwinner. Wherever he is—in airports and restaurants, before mass audiences, on television and radio, through tapes, videos, and literature—Dr. Jack Van Impe leads people to a personal experience with Jesus Christ. The ministry has documented the salvation of more than two million souls via its various outreaches.

He is "the walking Bible." Throughout his fifty-eight years of Christian service, Van Impe has consistently memorized key scripture passages, by both topic and reference. He has now committed more than 15,000 verses to memory, and extemporaneously quotes relevant biblical texts in his teaching and television commentary.

He is a respected scholar and acknowledged expert on Bible prophecy. From his teenage years, Jack was fascinated by the prophetic sections of the Bible and the historical record that confirmed its unerring accuracy. And over the past five decades, he has spent 90 thousand hours studying and interpreting the prophecies of the Word of God and their relevance to current and future world events.

A prolific writer and on-camera commentator, Van Impe's signature works include: *Revelation Revealed: Verse by Verse,* a 311-page explanation and interpretation of the last book of the Bible; *2001: On the Edge of Eternity,* up-to-date reports linking current world events to biblical prophecies; and *DANIEL Final End-Time Mysteries Unsealed,* a seven-hour, four video teaching series.

He is a master communicator. Jack Van Impe is now the most listened-to prophetic voice in the world. In addition to his own ministry outreaches, he has appeared on some 200 talk shows to share his Spirit-directed convictions, and has been asked to comment on significant world events by publications like *Time, Newsweek, U.S. News and World Report,* and scores of newspapers and other publications. He also distributes his own monthly prophecy forum, a newsletter called *The Van Impe Intelligence Briefing.*

He is a warm and witty friend. Although totally dedicated to his work—taking no time for hobbies or sports—and passionately intense in his ministry presentations, anyone around Jack for very long soon discovers that he is also a fun-loving person who loves to laugh. A natural-born story-teller, he delights in sharing humor and keeping conversations bubbling with his impromptu witticisms. Breaks from study are spent playing with the family cat, Fenica II, or doing light gardening, and he and Rexella occasionally enjoy having simple meals out with close friends.

I Must Be About My Father's Business —Luke 2:49

"Listen, Jack, the Lord is coming soon, and if we don't see you anymore here, we'll meet up there!"

Oscar Van Impe embraced his son, got into the family station wagon where his weeping wife was waiting, and slowly drove away. The vehicle was loaded with virtually all their earthly possessions—clothing and personal affects, an accordion, some Christian books and literature, and other items intended for use during an extended missionary trip to Belgium, the couple's homeland.

Tears streamed down Jack's face as he watched his parents—the only family he had ever known—drive away. The Korean War was going on, and the news coming out of Belgium and the rest of Europe reported growing political unrest. Would his loved ones be safe? Would he ever see them again?

In addition to his sense of separation and concern, young Jack felt the weight of responsibility for the family home in Detroit, for paying the monthly utility bills and operating expenses, and keeping the house maintained and in good repair. His parents had not been able to leave him any money at all—in fact, their mission was extremely under-funded and would require additional support from America.

Jack was a full-time Bible school student, working to pay his own tuition and living expenses. Believing in his parents' mission to witness for Christ in their homeland and win their unsaved families to the Lord, he unhesitatingly agreed to take on the heavy additional responsibilities.

He was eighteen years of age.

* * * * *

Jack Van Impe was not the usual 18-year-old. He had been performing before crowds of people as a musician since he was five. His father, a talented accordionist who played in Detroit's Belgian beer halls and nightspots, and for private gatherings and parties, started teaching Jack to read music when he was four. At five he was taking lessons and practicing an hour a day.

Then Oscar involved him in the family "act," having him play accordion duets with him and even tell a few jokes. Jack thrived on the attention, and quickly adapted to the rowdy, good-time atmosphere.

By age nine, Jack was already a seasoned "professional" on the night club circuit. But his musical repertoire had grown far beyond the lively polkas and bawdy drinking songs. A strict and demanding local accordion teacher named Peter Davey had been given the task of preparing a 9-year-old dynamo to be a concert accordionist. A perfectionist, Davey demanded hours of daily practice, and during lessons used a large, thick pencil to rap Jack's knuckles at each mistake.

The combination of talent and training produced a remarkable musician. And three years later, when first Oscar, then 12-year-old Jack, became born-again Christians, their music was "born again" too. The two were just as involved and enthusiastic in playing for the Lord as they had for the world. They played in church services and revival meetings, for Christian clubs and youth rallies—almost anywhere and anytime there was an opportunity.

JACK'S FIRST SERMON

During high school, Jack's pastor sensed that this young man was a minister in the making and arranged for him to preach his first sermon to all the youth of the church. Allotted 20 minutes to speak, the 15-year-old preacher wondered how he'd fit all his prepared material into such a short time. Six minutes later, he was done! Undaunted, Jack reshuffled his notes and went through them again—for another six minutes! So he prayed a closing prayer and sat down…with eight minutes to spare!

By the time Jack graduated from Detroit's Edwin Denby High School in 1948, he was a seasoned and experienced Christian worker. He was invited to appear with Billy Graham at a Youth for Christ meeting in Canada, playing his accordion. The result was a deluge of invitations to minister that kept him booked solid for the next year. That summer he traveled as crusade musician with evangelist Leonard Thompson, ministering in Michigan, Ohio, and Illinois.

Soon after his parents left for Belgium, Jack rented the house to a dependable couple, reserving a room for himself. This move both provided income and lessened personal responsibility. With the honorariums received from his many musical appearances, Jack had adequate income to cover his expenses… and even to help support his family's mission to Belgium.

Jack began devoting full attention to his studies at Detroit Bible College (now William Tyndale College) and to evangelizing the unreached. He was a straight "A" student who was not tardy or absent a single time in high school. His "A" average, with two exceptions, continued in college. His musical talent and effectiveness in sharing his Christian testimony created many opportunities for him to present the gospel.

He was completely confident that he was doing what he was supposed to do. Not only was he following in his earthly father's footsteps in using his talent for the Lord, but he also was emulating the example of Jesus in being diligent in carrying out his calling and commission to be about his Heavenly Father's business.

The Walking Bible

Mention any key doctrinal position or prophetic truth and wonder where it is in the Bible…

…mistakenly attribute a Shakespearean quote or an old farmer's saying as a scripture verse…

…ask where a particular Bible passage may be found…

…request additional references that mention a particular topic or truth…

…and Jack Van Impe can and will respond. He knows *all* the verses that relate to *every* key Bible doctrine. He knows the familiar quotations people often cite that *aren't* in the Bible. And he can quote—from memory—some 15,000 scripture verses by subject and in chronological order from Genesis to Revelation.

Hearing him cite dozens of relevant prophetic scriptures in his impromptu television commentaries on current news development is an ongoing source of fascination for viewers from week to week. And those who videotape the telecast and double-check Van Impe's memory by looking up the verses cited are amazed at his phenomenal accuracy.

Some people have attributed his amazing memorization ability as a divine gift. "Not so," he replies.

Others think he has a photographic mind. "Wrong again," he insists.

DESIRE, DISCIPLINE, AND DEDICATION

What then is the secret of the "Walking Bible's" amazing accomplishment? "Hard work," he declares. The keys to his success are desire, discipline, and dedication.

One source of inspiration to learn the Bible was a Bible school instructor, Dr. David Allen. Able to quote hundreds of verses, this experienced minister taught Bible and doctrinal development by comparing biblical texts, always giving the Word of God itself priority over theory and opinion. He made the Bible come alive to Jack and his fellow students.

One of Oscar Van Impe's legacies to his son when he left for his mission to Belgium was a pack of 500 cards containing scripture verses catalogued by doctrinal truth. The Bible verses were typed on one side of the cards, the book and verse references on the other side, along with the topic or subject. Jack found it to be easier and more effective to memorize verses by topic rather than in chapter order.

Carrying several cards with him at all times, he used every spare moment to go over and over the verses, repeating the verse and its reference at least seven times a day. Jack even propped cards up on the steering wheel of the car to review while waiting at traffic lights.

Van Impe was amazed at the impact on his life of memorizing Bible verses. First, he noticed a definite

difference in sensing the presence of God in every situation. Whether facing temptation or trial, the verses hidden in his heart seemed to come to mind just when he needed encouragement and strength.

His growing knowledge of the Word of God began to change his preaching. Rather than relying on stories and illustrations, he began reinforcing every point of his presentation with word-for-word recitations of the great proof texts of the Bible.

ENCOUNTERS WITH CRITICS

Later, having so much of the Bible committed to memory equipped Van Impe for encounters with critics and opponents. Representing the Michigan Sunday School Association in a radio-broadcast debate with an atheist, Van Impe quoted more than 500 verses in the first two hours of the encounter!

The moderator of a radio call-in show in Illinois had Jack Van Impe as a guest, and announced his intention to "tear the evangelist to shreds." Claiming to believe only the Old Testament, he started his attack by rejecting the Trinity, saying, "I can't accept the three-headed God of Christianity."

"Well, sir," said Jack, "I'll show you what that part of the Bible has to say about the Trinity." Starting with Genesis 1:1 at the first mention of God, he noted the plural form of the Hebrew word, *Elohim,* and marched on through the Old Testament books, listing numerous references to the Father, Son, and Spirit, including various verses in Proverbs, Psalms, and Zechariah.

At that point, the distressed moderator decided it was time to open the program to the calls of listeners!

On a network TV station in Philadelphia, Jack debated a college professor. The program started with a "put down," the announcer telling viewers the debate was between a fundamentalist and an intellectual. But after twelve minutes of being bombarded with Bible verses, the professor surrendered. Van Impe used the remainder of the time to share his testimony.

"WE HAVE ANOTHER MARTIN LUTHER ON OUR HANDS"

One of the earliest benefits of Jack's scripture memorization came during his preparation for ordination to the gospel ministry. Originally he had felt that his field of ministry would be music, utilizing his skill as an accordionist. But as he began to study and memorize the scriptures, the Word of God started burning in his soul and he began to recognize that preaching would indeed be a vital part of his service for the Lord. As a result, he requested ordination to the gospel ministry.

By this time he had memorized all 500 of the Bible verses his father had left behind on cards, already categorized by doctrinal position. This was an enormous help as Jack prepared himself for his ordination examination. He laid out his beliefs before the 11-man ordination council, using notes in stating the doctrines of the Bible, but quoting all the verses on which the doctrines are based in machine gun style, from memory.

The examining ministers were immediately aware of the discipline and hard work involved in making such a presentation. So thorough was the young candidate's coverage of Bible doctrine that the council thought only one question necessary. Dr. W. S. Hottel, the chairman of the group, asked, "Jack, do you really believe what you have just told us you believe?"

"Yes, sir, I certainly do, with all my heart."

"Gentlemen," said Dr. Hottel, "we have another Martin Luther on our hands. Let's ordain him!"

The council unanimously concurred, and the service of ordination was held that evening. It was now official. The call of God to His servant had been recognized by men of God and by the church. And when Detroit Bible College graduated Rev. Jack Van Impe a short time later, the foundational equipping of this dedicated and dynamic young man for his life work in ministry was complete.

Driven By An All-Consuming Passion

Converted at age twelve with a genuine born-again experience, Jack Van Impe immediately dedicated his talent, time, and energies to God.

With his parents' encouragement, influence, and example to guide him, he began to witness and share his faith in every way possible. He distributed gospel tracts in his neighborhood, at school, and in various public places where large numbers of people passed by.

He learned how to share his testimony—of his family's transformation from nightclub entertainers to zealous Christian witnesses—and his personal change from tomato-throwing persecutor to sold-out-for-God disciple.

Jack's skill as an accordion virtuoso produced even more opportunities to perform as a Christian artist than in the secular world. Virtually every weekend, and many mid-week evenings, he was playing for churches, youth rallies, Bible clubs, and other Christian gatherings. In addition to playing music, often he would give part of his testimony, share Bible verses, or a short exhortation.

Throughout high school he spent virtually all his time outside the classroom pursuing souls… evangelizing!

In Bible college, the pattern continued. He joined with other students in witnessing teams. One of his friends, Gordon Lindsay, became a close co-laborer in reaching out to the lost, and they often ministered together. In the summer, they traveled as a team in one-night and week-long crusades.

FIRST MISSIONS TRIP

The next summer, Jack and another Bible school friend, Stanley Koenke, went to Belgium to do missionary work with Oscar and Louise Van Impe. They were sent by Youth For Christ as European Team number 102.

The young missionaries sailed for Belgium on the *R.M.S. NieuwAmsterdam,* a large passenger liner that crossed the Atlantic in ten days. True to his pattern, Jack practiced his accordion three to four hours daily on the voyage. The professional sounding music coming from his room caught the ear of a ship officer, who invited Jack to present a series of three concerts, one for each class of passengers on board.

During each concert in the ship's ballroom, Jack presented a variety of good music, including rousing marches, to enthusiastic applause. Then he took a few minutes to share his Christian testimony, relating his family's involvement in nightclub entertaining, drinking, and being saved from the emptiness of that life.

He and his fellow minister responded to an inquiry after the concert, opening the scriptures to a young woman and leading her to Christ.

Jack was also invited to preach for the Protestant services onboard the ship on Sunday, and ministered to about 400 people. Already the trip had become a true missionary outreach to present to the gospel.

In Belgium, there was a happy reunion with Oscar and Louise, and the chance to meet and get to know his relatives. Jack's parents had been hard at work, with several members of the family and neighborhood won to the Lord, and a new church started.

Teaming up with his parents, Jack and his friend, Stanley, toured several Belgian cities conducting street meetings and ministering wherever possible. Jack and Oscar attracted crowds with their excellent and lively accordion music, the two shared their testimony, and Stanley moved through the crowd passing out tracts and witnessing one on one.

school attendance of over 3,000. The telecast had a considerable impact on the Detroit area.

By this time, Jack was constantly in demand as a musician for the top speakers of the day. Billy Graham, George Beverly Shea, Cliff Barrow, and other well-knowns were all his platform associates in Youth For Christ rallies at the peak of that organization's strong ministry.

Advertising pieces for events where he appeared referred to his extraordinary music skill—"Jack Van Impe, the Flying-Fingered Accordionist." A Canadian writer from London, Ontario, described one of Jack's performances as "out of this world…tops, colossal, tremendous, indescribable." Such accolades could inflate the ego of anyone, and they were beginning to create an aura of pride in the young Van Impe.

Sometimes there was visible fruit from their efforts, and other days were discouraging. But the effort went on faithfully. There has been a lasting result from those days of ministry, and at least one member of the Belgian Van Impe family became a full-time minister.

FULL-TIME MINISTRY

Shortly after entering Detroit Bible College, Jack started appearing weekly on television with Dr. Robert Parr on "The America Back to God Hour." Dr. Parr was a dynamic preacher, pastor of one of the fastest-growing churches in America with Sunday

But not for long! On his way to a meeting where he was to perform, he lost control of his car while traveling at 65 miles per hour. It rolled over, landing on its top in a ditch. Jack was shaken but not injured, and instantly he recognized why this "mishap" had occurred. Hebrews 12:6 flashed through his mind—***For whom the Lord loveth he chasteneth, and scourgeth every son whom he receiveth.***

GETTING RIGHT WITH GOD

Jack crawled out and looked at the damage. The car was a total loss. He recalled that he'd been using his tithe money to make his car payments. That money was lost, along with all his personal investment, since the insurance was inadequate to cover the loss.

His expensive accordion was inside the overturned car, and he was not sure if it had been damaged. Suddenly he realized that he was at the end of himself, and needed most of all to get right with God.

A sizable crowd had gathered along the busy highway where his car had crashed, and the police had been called. But oblivious to the onlookers, a humbled, chastened young disciple knelt in the ditch beside the wrecked automobile and confessed his sins to the Lord. He felt a great load lift as he claimed God's promise of forgiveness, and he promised to turn from backsliding, to be faithful in his personal relationship with the Lord, and to study the Bible to be equipped to give its message to others.

It was no empty vow. From the moment he rose from his knees that day, through every day for the next fifty years, Jack Van Impe has been driven by an all consuming passion to carry out that roadside promise in every way possible. Like the Prophet Jeremiah, his heart has cried out, ***His word was in mine heart like a burning fire shut up in my bones*** (Jeremiah 20:9).

THE TENDER TOUCH

Rexella Van Impe —
Partner In Life and Ministry

And the Lord God said, "It is not good that the man should be alone; I will make him a help meet for him..."
—Genesis 2:18

An encourager and help mate. For the first twelve years of their marriage and ministry together, the Van Impes traveled to local church crusades up to 40 weeks a year, staying in the homes of pastors and church members. In addition to her personal ministry duties, Rexella encouraged Jack daily, prayed with him, kept him laughing to keep his spirits high, and assisted him with his Bible memorization. "I wouldn't be in the ministry today without her," says Dr. Van Impe.

The "first lady" of sacred music. An accomplished pianist, Rexella was well experienced in vocal and instrumental music when she met Jack. She grew up singing in church, was involved in music throughout high school, and studied at Bob Jones University in Greenville, South Carolina. In addition to being a superb vocal soloist, she also played for church crusade services if necessary or provided accompaniment for Jack's accordion artistry. Her inspired singing on crusade platforms, albums, and national television earned her the title of "first lady of sacred music."

Television anchor-woman and co-host. As co-producer of the weekly ministry telecast, "Jack Van Impe Presents," Rexella exudes warmth and enthusiasm as she reads current news headlines and skillfully sets the stage for her husband's extemporaneous commentary and prophetic interpretation. On earlier nationwide TV specials and weekly programs, she did interesting, intelligent on-camera interviews with more than 200 influential world leaders, Christian scholars, and well-known personalities.

Popular author and speaker. Rexella's inspirational articles for *Perhaps Today* magazine reach into multiplied thousands of homes, and are often reprinted by other publications. Author of nine positive, uplifting books, she is a woman of strong principles and opinions, which makes her a popular speaker for seminars and conferences.

Respected ministry leader. An active member of the nine-member board of Jack Van Impe Ministries International, Rexella helps direct the global outreaches of the ministry. In addition to her other duties, she is jointly responsible for the production of the ministry's teaching and evangelistic videocassettes, which cover a wide range of topics and vary in length from one to ten hours. She has been recognized by International Women in Leadership with the acclaimed "Outstanding Woman in Ministry" award, and by Religion in Media with the prestigious "Woman of God" Gold Angel award. She also has received four Doctors Degrees, including a PhD in Journalism. As a ministry team, Rexella and Jack have been selected by RIM 33 times to receive Silver Angel awards for excellence in media.

Whither Thou Goest, I Will Go...

The promotional flyer for the Pontiac Youth For Christ Rally highlighted two musical performers—"Jack Van Impe, Accordionist Supreme"... and "Rexella Shelton, Soloist."

> *...and where thou lodgest, I will lodge: thy people shall be my people, and thy God my God.*
> —Ruth 1:16

Like the accordionist, Rexella was no stranger to the platform. She and her brother, Bob, had been singing together since they were small children. Having grown up in the large and active First Baptist Church of Pontiac, Michigan, she was at ease singing before large audiences.

With already many years of full-time ministry experience, the young Rev. Jack Van Impe was spending much time in those days praying for a wife. He recalls he was doing just that while awaiting his slot on the program that evening when he heard soft footsteps and looked up to see Rexella Shelton headed for the center of the stage. He knew in an instant that his prayers had been answered!

He listened with rapt attention as she communicated the gospel song to the youthful crowd and explained in her testimony that she felt God was calling her to work in evangelism. When she turned to walk off the platform, her eyes met his. His earlier reaction was confirmed.

There was one slight problem—she was dating another fellow. Jack recalls that he decided to obey the Bible's injunction to "watch and pray"—watching them both and praying the Lord would remove the competition.

Apparently it worked. Several weeks later Rexella stopped dating the other boy. She explained to him that she knew he was not the man she would marry and ended their relationship. For Jack, the chase was on!

GET REXELLA!

Rexella's brother, Bob, was a friend of Jack's, serving as the announcer on the television program, "America Back To God." He was convinced that Jack was the man for his sister and used his influence to help prepare the way. He invited Jack to come over to his house for a visit.

Although designed to get Rexella better acquainted with Jack, the visit added another valuable member to the Van Impe "get Rexella" team. Rexella's father liked the promising young preacher-musician from the start, and voiced his approval.

Bob continued the campaign, inviting his sister to sing on the TV program, knowing that Jack would be playing his accordion on the same telecast. A few days later, Jack called Rexella for their first date, and she accepted. They attended a youth rally together. It was the Christmas holiday season.

Although she enjoyed Jack's company and was flattered by his romantic attention, Rexella was seriously attracted to Jack a couple of month's later after hearing him speak in the Sunday evening service at the North Detroit Baptist Church. She was moved by the evidence of God's hand on him.

"I'd been attracted at first by Jack's musical talent and outward appearance. I'd certainly noticed how handsome he was—he made me look twice! But after hearing him minister, I was even more impressed by his message. He spoke with authority—he *knew* the Word of God…and what it meant. I never expected such wisdom, depth, and maturity in such a young man just out of college.

"I also was taken by his humility—a quality that has never gone away. I sensed that behind his spiritual boldness there was almost a shyness about him.

LESSON FROM A WHEAT FIELD

"I have a favorite devotional story that reminds me of this quality in Jack. A farmer took his young son out into a field of ripe wheat. The boy looked around and wondered aloud by some stalks stood so straight and tall, while others were bent over, their heads drooping.

"The farmer plucked a stalk of each kind and knelt beside his son. 'Look closely,' he said, 'and learn an important lesson. The reason this stalk stands so straight is that its head is light and empty—it's almost worthless. The bent stalk, on the other hand, is bowed over because its head is full, loaded with beautiful, valuable grain!'

"From the beginning I noticed that this modest, humble young man seemed to realize that in bowing his head before God, he would be filled with the fruit of knowledge."

BE SURE!

Devotion to God was supremely important to Rexella. Although born into a Christian home and reared in an active, vital church environment, there came a time in her developing years when she suffered the throes of doubt.

After singing in a church service, when she was almost 17, she left the church, obviously upset. Finding his daughter out on the parking lot by family car, weeping, Rex Shelton sought the source of her distress.

"Oh, Dad," she sobbed, I've deceived my own heart. I've deceived our pastor, and you, and the whole church. I have known *about* the Lord all my life, but I don't really know Him."

Resisting the temptation to soothe the feelings of his brokenhearted daughter, Rexella's father acted wisely. "Be sure, Rexella," he said, "be sure!"

Soon afterward, her brother, Bob, led Rexella to Christ. When the assurance of salvation came, it never wavered again. For most of her life, Rexella had been preparing herself for a life of Christian service. An extremely talented singer, she studied music and became an accomplished pianist. Throughout high school and college she prepared herself to be well equipped for ministry in evangelism.

THE COURTSHIP AND THE CALL OF GOD

Jack and Rexella recall that their courtship was a relationship built around spiritual things. Most of their dates were to services where he was preaching and where she ministered musically, either vocally or on the piano. They always prayed together at some time during an evening out.

While both were serious minded, they also loved to laugh and have a good time. Their time together was high spirited and happy, with lots of hilarity. But both were keenly aware of a distinct call of God on their lives.

Jack's ministry kept him away from home a considerable amount of time, a difficult situation for a young couple in love. But when apart, their letters were filled with love and conversation about the ministry and their future.

Only six months after their first date, Jack felt it was time to propose. On a warm summer evening, he and Rexella came home from a prayer meeting and found the front room of the house empty. The moon was shining into the large picture window and Jack saw the setting as ideal for his important question.

Taking Rexella's hand and leading her near the window, he said, "I remember your testimony at the youth rally where we met—about your call to evangelistic work. Would you join me in a lifetime partnership, serving the Lord together? I love you and would like to have you for my wife." Taking a modest diamond ring from his pocket, he offered it to her.

"I love you, Jack," she answered softly, "and I'll accept your ring tonight, but tomorrow you must get the approval of my parents."

It was a wonderful and unforgettable moment. Jack walked out into the pleasant moonlight a happy man. In a few months, Rexella would be his wife.

WEDDING BELLS

The wedding was set for August 21st. It was a large affair, with 800 guests. Jack stood at the back and greeted each one at the door to the church as if he were welcoming them to a revival meeting. His only regret was that his parents were still in Belgium and unable to attend.

Following the beautiful ceremony, the groom played his accordion and gave his personal testimony at the reception. Both Jack and Rexella wanted their wedding and reception to carry the message that would be the center of their lives and the purpose of their existence.

The next day the newlyweds departed for Mackinac Island, a beautiful resort in upper Michigan. The first night of their trip they stopped at a Bible conference in Traverse City, a picturesque place on the shore of Lake Michigan. Jack was to speak there on Saturday night at a youth rally before proceeding to their honeymoon destination.

Following the Saturday night rally, the honeymooners were asked to remain another day. Since it would be Sunday, and they wanted to attend church services somewhere anyway, they consented. Sunday brought another plea to remain the next day and assist in the

meetings, for which they would be furnished a lovely lakeside cottage and given *total* privacy. Again, they accepted, and moved "temporarily" into the cottage.

At 5:00 a.m. on Monday, the speaker for the week (Dr. John Zoller) knocked at the cottage door and asked the honeymooning preacher if he would like to go fishing! Their privacy was not quite "total."

The Van Impes never made it to Mackinac Island. They spent the entire week playing, singing, and speaking in the services at the Bible conference. Perhaps allowing ministry to take precedence over unfulfilled honeymoon plans was significantly symbolic, giving a preview of their life together.

However, the honeymoon goes on.

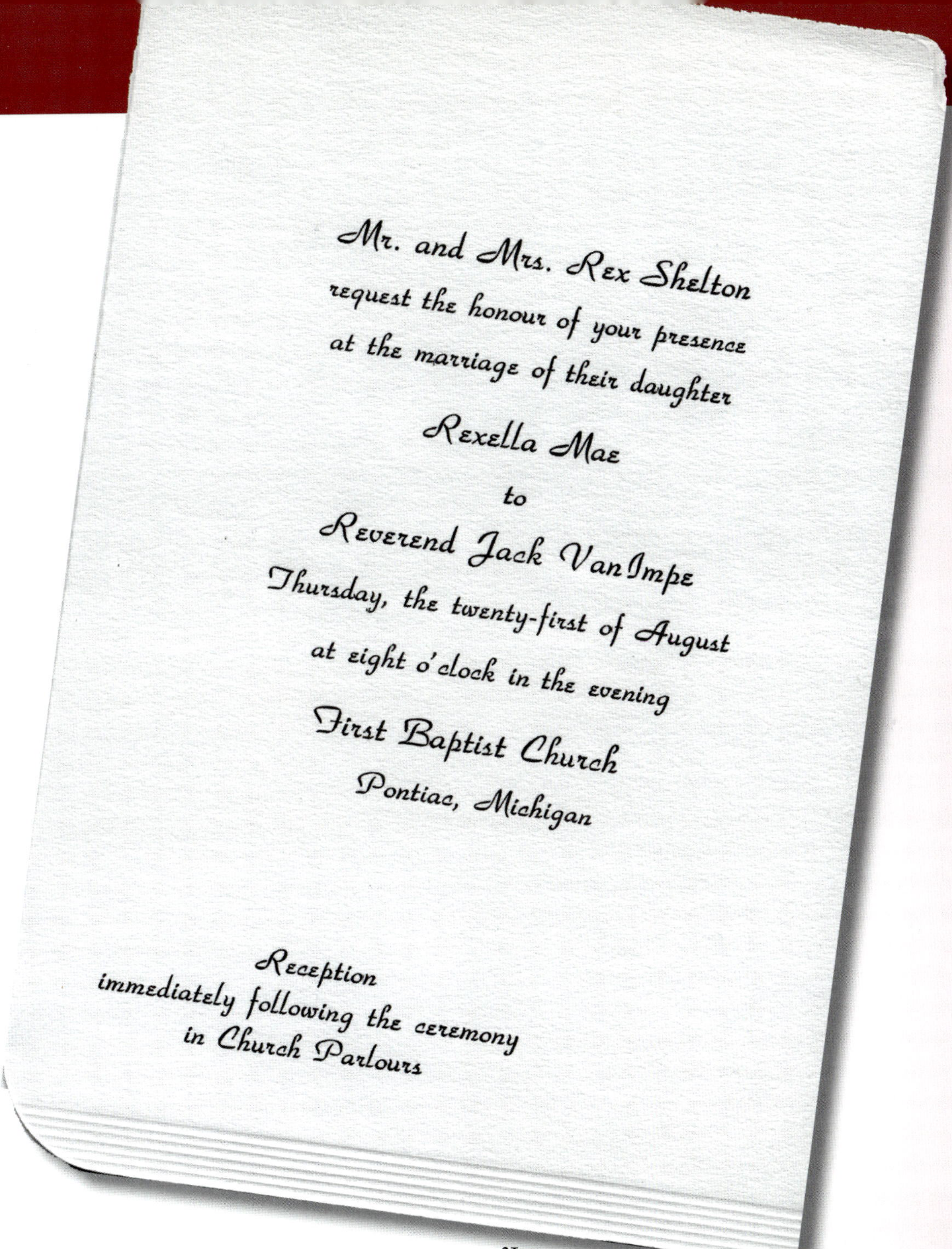

Mr. and Mrs. Rex Shelton
request the honour of your presence
at the marriage of their daughter

Rexella Mae

to

Reverend Jack VanImpe

Thursday, the twenty-first of August

at eight o'clock in the evening

First Baptist Church

Pontiac, Michigan

Reception
immediately following the ceremony
in Church Parlours

Ambassadors for Christ

What On Earth Are We Doing?

A foundation had been established for a lifetime ministry. Convictions were beginning to solidify! Their names were becoming known in an ever-widening area.

After settling into the Van Impe home (now rented from Oscar and Louise, who were still in Belgium) the new Rev. and Mrs. Jack Van Impe launched their evangelistic ministry together in Bay City, Michigan.

Since they were equipped to provide both music and the message in their meetings, they had decided to travel under a name they hoped would convey the image of a team. They called themselves "Ambassadors for Christ."

Although a good title, both biblical and descriptive, it never caught on with the public. In Bay City, and across the nation, they would be known affectionately as "Jack and Rexella."

The Van Impes delivered quite a concert each evening, with Rexella singing old and new songs of inspiration, and Jack conveying his enthusiasm for life and the gospel through his exciting accordion stylings. His sermons were loaded with Bible verses and delivered in a fiery evangelistic style that demanded attention and produced results.

The first crusade set a pattern that developed again and again through the years. The warm-hearted young people captured the hearts of those in the local congregation and the size of the crowd increased throughout the week.

Van Impe still marvels over the public response to their ministry in those early years. "We were so young," he says, "yet people accepted us and the meetings kept growing."

THE BLESSING OF THE LORD

There were reasons for that acceptance and enthusiasm. Both he and Rexella demanded excellence of themselves. They were human and happy enough for people to take them to their hearts. There was nothing fake about them at all. They had come to serve the Lord, to win souls, to revive the church.

Rexella recalls being amazed at the love and compassion she saw pouring from her husband as he ministered. "How often I have seen him weeping over the people he was preaching to, truly caring about their needs. And even when he was dead tired after preaching, he stayed after each service to meet people. Together we would counsel those with questions, offer encouragement, pray for special needs, and sign Bibles and share personal fellowship with individuals."

Those who attended those first meetings recognized and understood the unique quality of the Van Impes and spread the word. The results were predictable. The blessing of the Lord was upon their efforts.

In one of their early meetings, they went to a tiny church where only sixteen people showed up for their first service. The Van Impes ministered enthusiastically to that handful of people. The next night the crowd had

doubled! And it doubled again the next night. By the last night, 150 people crowded into the small building, and there was a glorious spirit of revival and renewal.

LIFE ON THE ROAD

Rexella says the first year in evangelism was a great learning experience, starting in Bay City. For the next twelve years she and Jack would live the greater share of their lives in the homes of others. In those days, it was customary for the evangelist to stay in the home of the pastor or a church member, which provided little privacy.

On the first night of that nomadic existence, she felt insecure and insisted that Jack pile the bedroom furniture in front of the door so no one could break into their room. Obediently, he moved several heavy items to make a barricade so Rexella could relax and sleep safely. All was well until Jack became ill in the night and needed to get out of the room to the bathroom in a hurry. All the furniture had to be hastily moved before he could get out of Rexella's "fortress." She never again demanded such tight security.

Living in other's homes meant that they were with people all the time, with little time alone. Being young and full of fun, Jack and Rexella usually had conversations long into the night about humorous and interesting things that had happened during the day. This necessitated whispering and laughing in hushed tones so as not to disturb their hosts. They became so accustomed to stifling noise that on one of their rare days at home in Detroit they found themselves going about the house conversing in whispers. When it dawned on them what they were doing, they broke up in peals of laughter.

Following the Bay City meeting, other openings in music and evangelism kept the Van Impes *busy*. This is a word that has remained to this day. For the first year or so they spent about half their time providing music for other evangelists and at special rallies and conferences, and the other half conducting their own crusades.

DESTINATION: BELGIUM

Since Rexella had never met her husband's parents, they began planning a trip to Belgium. It seemed a wonderful opportunity to get the whole family together and offered valuable experience in missionary work, while aiding Oscar and Louis in their ministry. Three months in the summer were set aside for the European journey. Jack cashed in his life insurance policy to pay for the trip.

They arranged their meetings to work their way across the country, ending in a wonderful 17-day crusade with Rev. Dick Robinson in Atlantic City, New Jersey. The meeting was very productive, with record attendance and a wave of revival that swept the congregation from the youth to the oldest member.

The Van Impes departed from Hoboken, New Jersey, on the *Maasdam* for a 10-day crossing to Belgium. For Rexella, it seemed like an eternity as she was seasick all the way. In spite of her discomfort, however, they were able to minister during the trip. Getting acquainted with a missionary couple on board, Jack and Rexella worked with them in a number of gospel meetings on the ship. Again, Jack was able to share his testimony with the passengers and use the trip itself as a means of missionary work.

Flags were flying when Jack and Rexella arrived in Rotterdam. The Van Impe family was waiting at the dock, holding the Belgian and American flags. It was another glad reunion for Jack and his parents and a special occasion as he introduced Rexella to all the relatives. Oscar and Louise were overjoyed at their son's choice of a wife and recognized immediately that God had arranged this marriage. Their attractive daughter-in-law was an answer to their prayers.

In getting acquainted with her husband's family, Rexella came to an understanding of the forces that had shaped the man she loved. Oscar's boundless enthusiasm and Louise's quiet nature seemed so perfectly blended in their son. She was grateful for the opportunity to meeting and getting to know them.

BIRTH OF A VISION

Jack and Rexella enjoyed assisting Jack's parents in their missionary work in Belgium, and also accompanied them on a tour of several European countries, including France, Holland, Spain, Italy, Switzerland, and Germany. The excursion was relaxing for the tired missionaries and gave the younger Van Impes a vision of the spiritual hunger of Europeans. The concern generated on that trip never left them, and was, in part, responsible for their burden to carry the gospel to the entire world by all means possible.

On board the ship carrying them back home, Jack and Rexella celebrated their first wedding anniversary. It had been an eventful year of love and learning. A foundation had been established for a lifetime ministry. Convictions were beginning to solidify. Their names were becoming known in an ever-widening area. They were returning to an increasingly busy schedule of music and crusade work.

Doing the Work of an Evangelist

Arriving home meant being on the road again. Youth For Christ was still one of their most important contacts for meetings. Jack was being used in giant rallies as the featured musician. A number of celebrities had been converted in those years and were being promoted at YFC rallies as speakers. The "big name" was important, but good music rounded out a program. Jack Van Impe, with his high-energy, technically-brilliant accordion styling and solid spiritual testimony was often the featured musical artist.

Jack was also in demand to play at Bible conferences to complement the ministries of well-known Bible teachers. Program brochures billed him as "The Nation's No. 1 Gospel Accordionist."

In addition to their musical appearances and week-long local church meetings, the Van Impes also were being noticed and invited to minister in larger events. The Summer Bible Conference of the First Baptist Church of Atlantic City, New Jersey, used Rev. Van Impe for both music and preaching.

Although beginning to mature as a preacher, Jack still became somewhat self-conscious at times. On one occasion when a well-known pastor attended his meeting, the young evangelist got completely rattled. Preaching on the return of the prodigal son, he had the father calling for the servants to come and place shoes on his hands and a ring on his feet!

Early in his ministry, Jack made a decision about the public invitation given at the end of evangelistic services. He knew there were gimmicks and tricks some preachers used to get as many people as possible to come forward. Jack felt some of these methods bordered on dishonesty and resolved that his invitation to the lost and backslidden would be straightforward and to the point, with no traps. Pastors across the country soon learned they trust him to handle this sensitive part of a meeting with reverence and good taste.

Being faithful to the fundamentals, both biblically and ethically, produced good results. Churches invited the Van Impes back to minister again and again. New and lasting friendships were formed with ministers and laymen.

IT'S NOT ALL SERIOUS

In a church in St. Petersburg, Florida, the pastor's 7-year-old son was fascinated by Jack's expertise on the accordion. The minister told Jack how his boy went around at home imitating the "bellows shake" he'd seen Van Impe perform, a difficult accordion technique which was very entertaining to the audience. That night Jack repeated the story to the congregation and said, "Jimmy, you keep that up and you'll be able to play the accordion one day."

After service that night, little Jimmy went to his father and said, "If that evangelist embarrasses me one more time I'm quitting the church!"

* * * * *

On another occasion, in a meeting in Flint, Michigan, Jack walked out on the platform in front of the choir and bent over to pick up his accordion. Suddenly there was the frightening sound of ripping fabric. The seat of his trousers had given way. Because he was next on the program—to play and then preach—there was no time to go change. So he slipped on his raincoat.

"I'm sorry, friends," he said, "I just had a little accident here." And he wore the raincoat for the rest of the service. That embarrassment kicked off an immediate diet and exercise program that took off excess pounds!

* * * * *

During a crusade in Pasadena, California, Jack was invited to speak at an Easter sunrise service up in the Richmond-Wally Creek area. Knowing it would be very chilly outdoors, friends loaned him a set of "long johns" woolen underwear to wear under his suit. And he was comfortable during the shivery-cool early morning celebration.

Then the ministerial team flew directly back down to Pasadena to be in the regular Easter morning worship service. There was no time to change out of the "long johns," and in the warm, upper-80s temperature, Jack got so hot he nearly fainted as he ministered.

FIELD CONDITIONS

The "romance" of evangelistic life wore off pretty quickly. The travel, the "limelight," and the admiration and appreciation of the crowds, were more than offset by the long hours, constantly strange surroundings, the lack of privacy, and abysmally poor pay. Had both Jack and Rexella not looked upon evangelism as a divine calling, they might not have survived the rigors of those first years in local church crusades.

In a Texas church, the pastor had moved just before the crusade, leaving the parsonage empty. The church board, therefore, simply threw a mattress on the floor and told Jack and Rexella to make that their home for their time with them. The temperature was 98 degrees most of the week and there were no screens on the windows. They were nearly eaten alive by bugs. It was a week to remember—or forget!

One poorly organized pastor hadn't arranged any lodging for the Van Impes before the crusade and on the first day of the meetings asked for help in housing from the congregation. A visiting couple volunteered their tiny home. They had but one bedroom and so it was necessary for Jack and Rexella to sleep in the kitchen. There they watched from their bed each morning as their host and hostess ate breakfast at five o'clock before leaving for work.

During the years of local church meetings, the Van Impes often ate one meal a day in the homes of different church members. While they have many fond memories of good fellowship around tables where they became a part of Christian family circles, there also were some meals they'd rather forget. Jack still gets groans at the recollection of having chicken for dinner seventeen days in a row!

FINANCIAL TRIALS

On one cross country tour, the "Ambassadors for Christ" were on the road for sixteen long weeks without a break. They'd close one meeting on Sunday night, drive to the next city on Monday, and start the crusade that night or the next. It was a grueling pace. At the end of the sixteen weeks of conducting meetings in small home mission churches and paying for their travel and personal expenses, they had made a grand total of $80.

Jack credits Rexella for their happiness and ability to survive financially as they were starting out. "She was always willing to sacrifice and do without new things," he says. "It hurt me to see my wife struggling along with me under such adverse conditions. But she never complained—instead she kept encouraging me as we trusted the Lord to meet our needs."

Rexella recalls times when she and her husband would labor long hours and pour out their very lives to help bring revival to a church. "We'd sing and play and preach and pray, night after night. Often we'd see attendance double or triple until the church was packed, and as much as half the membership would make decisions for Christ.

> *Had both Jack and Rexella not looked upon evangelism as a divine calling, they might not have survived the rigors of those first years in local church crusades.*

"Sometimes pastors would promise us one or two love offerings for the week. But when they'd see the big crowds giving generous offerings, they didn't want to keep their word. They saw a chance to get extra money to pay off back debts for the church, or some other project. So at the end of the week, we'd get maybe $100 or so—for the two of us, for ministering in every service.

"Jack would be so hurt, feel so betrayed. We had rent and utilities to pay at home, and we were trying to save up enough to make a down payment on our own place.

Then, instead of receiving the offering we were promised, we'd get barely enough to put gas in the car, pay for our laundry and cleaning, and for other personal expenses.

"Weary and brokenhearted, Jack would say, 'Why are we staying out here, Rexella? People don't appreciate what we're doing. We can't even make a living. Maybe we should go home and find other jobs!'

"'Come on, now,' I'd say. 'God has called us into evangelism, and we are going to stay in evangelism. Souls are being saved. People are being blessed. We're where we're supposed to be. Don't worry, honey, we'll find a way to make it work.'

HIS GRACE IS SUFFICIENT

"So we'd go on. Jack would spend hours praying and studying, practicing his accordion, working on scripture memorization. We did our mail on the road, too, answering letters, acknowledging special gifts, working on travel itineraries. Also, I helped type hundreds—thousands of Bible verses on index cards for Jack's memory program.

"There were lots of lonely times. When you're that alone, only God can fill the void. Whatever the needs—emotional, spiritual, whatever—God supplied them all through prayer and the fellowship of the Holy Spirit. I think those were the days when God put us through the fire to see if we were going to be faithful and hold on.

"I turned to my Bible for strength and encouragement—I read through it, Genesis to Revelation, many times. The Word became very dear to me. That's when Christ was formed in me and became so real and such a dear Friend. Hebrews 12:2 became my anchor—*Looking unto Jesus the author and the finisher of our faith*. We learned right away not to look to or depend on men—we had to 'look to Jesus' and work as unto the Lord."

Rexella pauses, a faraway look in her eyes. "Those were tough times, but wonderful times, too. We had no one to turn to, no friends or family around. We only had God and each other. But I'm telling you, *that was enough!*"

Stir the Saints...Save the Sinners

From the beginning of his full-time ministry, Jack made the Bible the central theme of his message. Rather than emphasizing dramatic stories or emotion-packed illustrations, he focused on two themes: *What does the Bible say? And How should this truth affect your life?*

Van Impe's consummate artistry on the accordion could easily have catapulted him to fame and fortune as a musical entertainer. His good looks, technical brilliance, flamboyant arrangements, and flashy style made him a popular performer wherever he went, and brought invitations for "show business" appearances and recording opportunities.

But Jack was sure of his calling to proclaim the gospel of Christ. And as much as he loved music—even Christian and sacred stylings—he knew from the beginning that ministering the Word of God was to have primacy in his life. As he explained to the pastors at his ordination, music was a useful tool to attract a crowd so that he could preach the gospel to a greater number of people.

After a couple of years of appearing before huge crowds in rallies and conferences as the featured musician and conducting his own local church crusades in smaller communities, Van Impe began to sense that God was speaking to him about making his preaching the most important part of his work.

MUSICIAN OR EVANGELIST?

He was invited to play his accordion at a large gathering of Christian musicians in Pasadena, California. Phil Kerr of "Monday Night Musicale" fame, had selected him as guest soloist for a great banquet for 2,500 musicians from across the nation. The honored appearance turned out to be a nightmare. At the height of his performance, in the middle of playing "Wonderful Grace of Jesus," the middle C-sharp key fell off his accordion and fell at his feet.

The host, Phil Kerr, tried to make a joke out of the mishap, and the guests roared with applause and laughter, thinking it was a planned joke. But for Jack, given to perfection in his work, it was a disaster as he left the banquet in humiliation.

Some months later Phil Kerr invited Van Impe to appear on his "Monday Night Musicale" program. He recognized the talent of the young accordionist and wanted to give him another chance. Jack accepted the invitation, but a few days before the performance, he was involved in a freak accident that cut his finger to the bone. Although there was no permanent damage, playing for Kerr's program was out of the question, and the opportunity at Pasadena ended forever.

DAY OF DECISION

Others might have interpreted the two incidents as unfortunate coincidences, but for Jack they confirmed what he had been feeling in his heart. The night of the accident, he made a covenant with the Lord that he would not accept any more invitations only to play the accordion. All future engagements would have to include the opportunity to preach the gospel.

When Jack made his decision known, some friends felt he was making a mistake. Many great opportunities would be closed to him. The Youth For Christ invitations would end. Well-known evangelists would stop using him in their meetings. His ministry seemed sure to be curtailed.

For the next few years the predictions of his friends proved true. But while some large platforms were closed, many smaller churches were looking for evangelistic teams like Jack and Rexella and doors continued to open for them. They accepted the humblest places as their special field of service and gave of themselves unreservedly. And God blessed them.

Small churches were packed to capacity time and again. Revival came in out-of-the-way places. Churches sometimes had as many conversions as they had members. People around the nation began to hear of a young husband and wife evangelistic team that packed church buildings with hungry-hearted people and left solid conversions in the wake of their meetings.

MOUNTAINTOPS AND VALLEYS

In a church in Richmond, California, revival came as the youth of the church stayed on their knees in prayer until midnight each night of the crusade. There were 102 conversions during the week.

One Michigan pastor scheduled the Van Impes for a meeting and was startled and overjoyed when half his membership came forward to be saved on the first Sunday!

Another church in that area was revolutionized during a Van Impe crusade by the conversion of five deacons who made up the entire church board.

Revival broke out in a Detroit church while Jack was speaking in Sunday school. There was such a response to the invitation to that message that the move of God continued on through the morning service. Scores were saved and about eighty percent of the congregation made significant spiritual decisions.

Then there were the "valley" experiences.

Some churches were poorly prepared, with no advertising or promotion, and inadequate prayer support. Sometimes the meeting was scheduled just because it was time for the annual revival, or the denomination required it. In these cases there was generally little effort or cooperation from the membership or the pastor.

On one such occasion, God poured out revival despite the lack of preparation. On the first week night service, 35 members of the congregation came to the Lord. The evening was an exciting outpouring of fire and faith.

Oddly enough, the pastor missed the blessing. When Jack and Rexella arrived at the parsonage after counseling the converts by themselves, they found the minister and his wife in front of the TV enjoying pop and potato chips. They'd slipped out of the church immediately after the service to get home in time for a favorite program.

Arriving at one church for a meeting, a member advised the Van Impes that if the pastor invited them to play Ping-Pong it would be best to let him win. Thinking this was just idle talk, Rexella enthusiastically accepted the minister's challenge to a game the next day. Apparently the layman's warning had been born out of experience. When she handily won the match, the pastor refused to speak to her for the rest of the week.

* * * * *

In an Ohio crusade that started on Tuesday night, many members of the church were absent all during the week. On Saturday, Jack went to the post office to mail a package and found a dozen other patrons in line ahead of him. He stepped to one side to look at the line and decide if he had time to wait or not.

A man in front of him growled, "What do you think you're doing? You can't cut in front of me."

"I'm not getting ahead of you, sir, I'm just seeing how many are already waiting."

"Don't give me that or I'll push your face in," was the angry reply.

The next morning when Jack turned to look at the choir, the angry postal patron was on the front row, now pale with shame. He was a deacon in the church! To his credit, he came to the evangelist with tears and they prayed together after the service.

"DON'T PREACH ABOUT THAT!"

A few pastors tried to tell Jack what to preach. What they didn't know was that attempting to tone down Van Impe was like trying to keep a bomb from exploding. One minister talked to Jack on Saturday afternoon before he was to share his testimony. "Don't get carried away talking about worldliness," the preacher said. "If you do, everyone visiting from our community will think we're squares."

That night—after Jack's *extra strong* emphasis on worldliness—the pastor's daughter was the first to come forward. Another convert in that service was a doctor, the pastor's personal physician. Still rejoicing after the service, the doctor asked Rexella, "I wonder how much is owed on this church?" She directed his attention to a wall chart that indicated the remaining balance of a building fund drive. "Oh, good," he said, "I'll write a check for that amount right now!"

It was a worthwhile lesson for the troubled preacher who had been so concerned about the reaction of the community.

TIMES OF BLESSING

The years in single church crusades introduced the Van Impes to many new friends. Since the audiences were smaller, they were able to get personally acquainted with a greater percentage of the congregation. Many of these people still stay in regular contact with the Van Impes and pray faithfully for the ministry.

The Van Impes and countless friends across the nation remember great times of spiritual blessing in the local church meetings. For example, the Saturday night service in the Corning, New York crusade was postponed because of a blizzard. Everyone was disappointed because the crowds had been building toward that last meeting all week long.

Conducted on Sunday afternoon, the last service resulted in 14 conversions. Not one of those converted could have attended any evening meeting. And all 14 became faithful workers in that church.

In York, Pennsylvania, Pastor Ralph Boyer was burdened for his wayward son. When the Van Impes were in his church for a crusade, Jack and the pastor prayed long into the night for the young man, who at that time was an entertainer in nightclubs in Atlantic City, New Jersey.

When the miracle of salvation transformed the son, the Van Impes rejoiced with the family. The converted pastor's son in Dave Boyer, who now uses his singing talent for the Lord. The book and film, *So Long, Joey*, are accounts of his life and conversion.

TRANSITION TIME

Year after year, Jack and Rexella continued to criss-cross the United States and Canada in local church crusades. There was seldom a break between meetings, with the team being on the road some 40 weeks each year. They consistently broke attendance records. "Standing room only" crowds became the expected thing. Having to move to larger auditoriums to finish crusades became common.

In addition to his regular prayer and study time, Jack was now spending an average of two hours a day practicing his accordion, and another two hours working on his scripture memorization program. Because of this disciplined work schedule, the Van Impes had begun staying in hotels or motels, where they could have a bit more privacy.

By the mid-60s, many of the single church crusades were held in churches with several thousand members. Two crusades in the great Highland Park Baptist Church in Chattanooga, Tennessee, saw nearly 400 conversions. In Syracuse, New York, 1,000 came forward at the invitation. The Scranton, Pennsylvania crusade resulted in the largest attendance since the days of Billy Sunday.

As word of the growing crowds and unusual results in Van Impe crusades spread around the nation, Jack and Rexella found invitations for meetings growing beyond their ability to accept them. While they ultimately would conduct some 800 single church meetings, groups of churches were uniting to invite them to come for areawide crusades.

Jack Van Impe's uncompromising message and strict adherence to ethical principles had gained him a place of trust among Christian leaders throughout the nation. His ministry was producing multitudes of genuine conversions. Churches were being revived and helped.

Rexella, the perfect teammate, added a tender touch, and complemented his accomplished accordion work with heart-moving vocal solos and piano specials. All the ingredients were present for a ministry to millions.

And God was about to make it happen.

Letters We Love...
about the local church crusades

THANKS FOR FAITHFUL MINISTRY

I accepted Christ under your ministry in a meeting in Pennsylvania in 1955. Thanks so much for your faithful ministry over the years. We appreciate what you are doing now and especially enjoy your excellent videos.
—*D. & B. R., Holley, NY*

CONVERT IS NOW A MINISTER

I just wanted to let you know that my husband and son were saved under your ministry at Thomas Road Baptist Church years ago. My son is now a minister in Harrisburg, Virginia.
—*J. C., Evington, VA*

SON SAVED AT 15

My son went forward at one of your meetings when he was just 15 years old. He is now an assistant pastor at Hespeler Baptist Church.
—*E. M., Kingsville, Ontario, Canada*

ACCORDION SOLOIST

I was a member of the Salvation Army band many years ago when you came with your accordion as guest soloist at our Thanksgiving concert. We have been blessed through the years by your ministry and have obtained many of your tapes and books.
—*H. O., Somerset Center, MI*

FAMILY MEMBERS SAVED BEFORE HOMEGOING

Back in the 60s you came to Plainfield, New Jersey. My grandmother rededicated her life to Christ, and my dear father repented of his sins and accepted Christ as Saviour. Both of them are now with the Lord.
—*R. B., Pittstown, NJ*

HELPING SPREAD THE WORD

I attended one of your crusades in the Upper Peninsula of Michigan many years ago. Because of your ministry, I made a commitment that night to go into the ministry and help spread the gospel. I have now been pastoring for several years and more than 100 people have been saved because of that decision. You hold a special place in my heart—I wouldn't be in the ministry today had I not attended your crusade.
—*T. S., Coopersville, MI*

"IT'S GOOD TO HEAR YOU AGAIN"

We were saved when you were a guest speaker for a revival back in 1948. How it thrilled us to hear you play your accordion. We are so glad to be able to hear you again in our area.
—*C. & A. S., Bradenton, FL*

Letters We Love...
about the local church crusades

FRIENDS GAVE HEARTS TO THE LORD

Years ago, when you came to Saginaw, we took a friend and her daughter to hear you and they both gave their hearts to the Lord. That, in itself, has made your ministry very dear to our hearts. God bless you.

—D. S., Midland, MI

CONVERT NOW "CHURCH PLANTER"

My husband was saved at one of your rallies many years ago when he was just in junior high. Following your example, he began to memorize scripture while working in a factory. At age 28, he left his job and went to Bible college to prepare for full-time Christian service. We are now serving the Lord as church planters in the very needy mission field of rural America.

—D. G., Clearmont, WY

MOTHER, SON MAKE DECISIONS SAME NIGHT

I was privileged to be in the audience during your two visits to Mansfield. Although I thought I was a Christian, your messages made me stop and think. The same night I went forward to the altar, my youngest son went to the other end of the altar and we weren't sitting together. What a joyful night that was!

—Mrs. J. S., Ohio

UNFORGETTABLE NIGHT

I watch your program on TV every week. It's special because the Van Impes helped bring me to Christ. When you were preaching at First Baptist Church of Hollywood, I heard Jack play his accordion and preach and Rexella sang. It was a night I won't ever forget.

—M.C., Los Angeles, CA

SON SAVED AT JVI MEETING

We've kept track of you since you spoke in a meeting in our church in Minneapolis, Minnesota, in the 1960s. Our youngest son, Blair, and his wife, Diane, were saved at one of your meetings there. Then all four of us followed to hear you speak in a St. Paul meeting. Blair is still working for the Lord—witnessing and winning souls in Charlotte, North Carolina.

Two million stories could be printed from their combined efforts over the years. This would require volumes of books the size of an encyclopedia. God has anointed and empowered Jack and Rexella as two of the leading soul-winners of the 20th century.

49

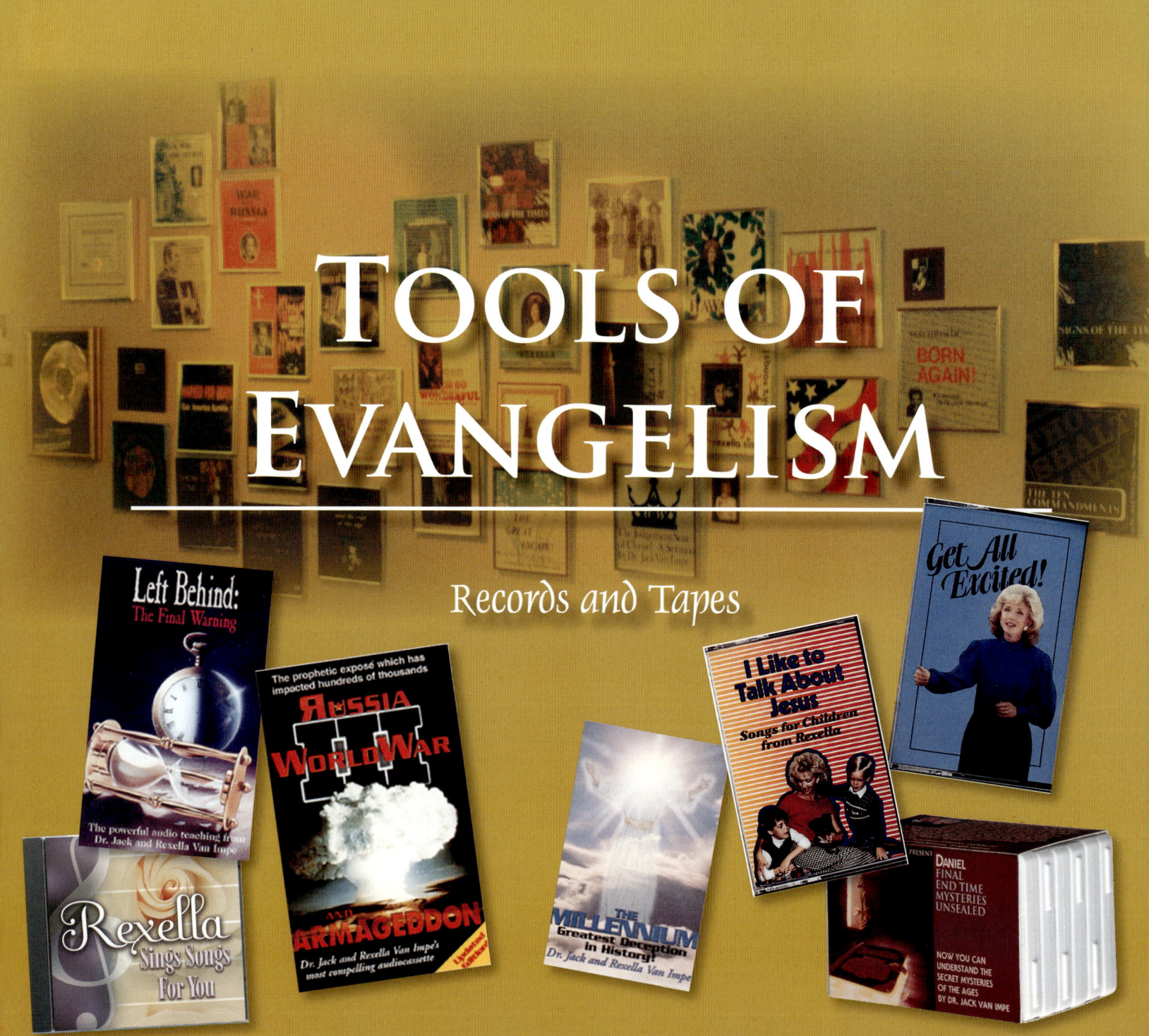

In 1969, at the time the Van Impes were shifting from single church meetings to areawide cooperative crusades, Dr. Van Impe had started preaching a compelling prophetic message. Entitled "The Coming War With Russia," the sermon had startling impact on each congregation that heard it.

After preaching it at Thomas Road Baptist Church of Lynchburg, Virginia, Jack was approached by the pastor, Jerry Falwell, a good friend who had received his doctorate from Tennessee Temple Schools on the same night as Van Impe. "Jack, you've got to record that sermon," said Falwell. "People everywhere need to hear that message."

At that time, making a sermon record seemed like a big undertaking and a radical step to Van Impe, and his uncertainty must have been obvious. So Falwell continued to persuade him, finally saying jokingly, "Look, if you don't put that message on a record, I'm going to!"

Making a recording was good advice. "The Coming War With Russia" was an instant best seller, remaining in demand for years. According to ministry estimates, the recorded message was responsible for the conversion of at least 10,000 people.

The success of this record dramatized the importance of producing and using recordings as tools for evangelism. So Dr. Van Impe began producing other sermon records with bold subjects, such as "The Judgment Seat of Christ," "Hell Without Hell," "Heaven," "Signs of the Times," "The Beginning of the End," "The Greatest Love Story Ever Told," and numerous others. These records found ready acceptance and became tremendously popular.

The Van Impes also began producing records of their musical presentations—his accordion stylings and her inspirational solos. These, too, were much in demand.

This new outreach helped multiply the effectiveness of the Van Impe's ministry, reaching tens of thousands with the gospel through recordings. In fact, the Van Impes later were presented with a gold record by Carroll and Lynda Rawlings of Artists' Recording Co. to hail the one million recordings they produced and distributed.

The Van Impes were quick to utilize the development of audio cassette tapes. Soon more than 100 of Dr. Van Impe's messages—including series of prophetic studies—were in distribution by the tens of thousands. Tapes have been distributed through public meetings, via radio and television, and through magazine and direct mail offers.

Also, thousands of tapes have been distributed overseas for use in scores of nations by missionaries, national ministers, and individuals. Only eternity will reveal the far-reaching harvest of souls won through the Van Impe's recordings.

Letters We Love...
about records and tapes

RECORD HELPED LEAD ME TO CHRIST

Your record, *"The Coming War With Russia,"* which you produced many years ago, was instrumental in my turning my life over to Christ—just four years ago. My mother had kept your record stored away for a long time, and I just happened to find it and play it. As a result, I took a Gideon Bible out of a motel room, read it for two weeks, and found Christ as my Saviour.

—*Rev. T.F., Canada*

FUTURE SON-IN-LAW SAVED

Yesterday we played your tape, *"You Must Be Born Again,"* for our future son-in-law. After it was over, I had the joy of leading him to the Lord.

—*H.V., East Hartford, Connecticut*

TRUCKER SHARES JESUS ON ROAD

I'm a trucker, and I spend about 90 percent of my time on the road passing the word on to others about Jesus Christ and Jack Van Impe Ministries. I have *"Revelation Revealed…Verse by Verse"* on cassette tape, and I just love it so much. I'm turning other truckers on to listening to you, and they are really fascinated by your ministry. I've learned so much from the items I've ordered—I plan to order every cassette you have in stock.

—*G.B., Cincinnati, Ohio*

NIGERIAN'S LIFE CHANGED BY TAPE

A friend gave me one of your tapes, and after listening to it I felt happy. It helped me accept Christ as my Savior. Thank God for using you to propagate the gospel of Christ to the world.

—*K.O., Nigeria*

INDIAN USES TAPES TO EVANGELIZE

I received your six cassettes containing wonderful sermons. I will go through each and translate it into my native language and use these messages to win my native people to Jesus. My church now has 200 members.

—*K.K., Andhra Pradesh, India*

TAPES GO CAMPING

We took your cassette series, *"Revelation Revealed"* on a recent camping trip and listened to them every night by the campfire. After hearing them two or three times, we are really beginning to get a grip on what it all means. Thank you for following the Holy Spirit's leading in making the tapes.

—*D. & T.D., Long Beach, California*

Letters We Love...
about records and tapes

OPENED MY EYES

The tapes have opened my eyes to so many scriptures and answered so many questions—questions there seemed to be no answers for. The gift you have from God certainly has been a blessing to me, as well as to millions. Your ministry has helped me so much.

—M.L., New York, New York

PARENTS SAVED

Last week my husband went to see his 75-year-old parents. When he got there, he played your tapes for them, then led both of his parents to the Lord Jesus Christ.

—Mrs. M.L., Burbank, Washington

TAPE BROUGHT SALVATION

I thought you'd be interested to know I was saved through one of your tapes, *"Hell Without Hell,"* in 1975.

—J.C., Schererville, Indiana

NEW FAMILY MEMBERS

Last October, three of us entered into the beautiful family of God. This was made possible by our grandmother giving us your tape called, *"The Signs of the Times."* Thank the Lord for saving our unworthy souls.

—K., P.K, & P.D., Owensboro, Kentucky

AFRICAN BLESSED

Recently a friend of mine received some of your cassettes which contained preaching and singing. He shared them with me and I am please to tell you that I have received Jesus Christ as my personal Saviour. I prayed to Him to forgive my sins. The cassettes help me praise and worship God.

—S.A., Ghana

Go Ye Into All The World

Reaching The Mission Field

In addition to making several ministry trips to Belgium, the homeland of Jack's parents, the Van Impes have obeyed the words of Jesus to go into all the world and preach the gospel. Their missions have taken them to virtually every spot in North America and into 50 countries.

Taking a break from their regular U.S. crusade circuit in 1967, Jack and Rexella made an evangelistic tour of South America. Most of the meetings were very successful one night rallies, but a longer crusade that ended on a tense note was held in the Panama Canal Zone.

The crowds grew so large that it was necessary to move the meeting out of doors into a valley stadium, surrounded by hills. The university in the Canal Zone had been closed the week before because of communist influence and there was great unrest. Jack was preaching on "The Coming War With Russia," a topic that concerned the sponsors responsible for the young evangelist's safety. Anyone waiting in the hills would have found him an easy target.

Churches in the Philippines hosted crusades in three cities during January, 1975. Services were conducted in Cebu City, Manila, and Baguio, with dramatic results. The Van Impes saw 6,514 come to Christ in the Filipino meetings.

In recognition of his work in evangelism, Dr. Van Impe was selected as a speaker for the World Congress of Fundamentalists, which took place June 15-22, 1976, in Edinburgh, Scotland. Two thousand delegates, representing every continent, attended. Dr. Van Impe presented a paper on "The Fundamentalist and Evangelism."

In addition to personally traveling around the world, for years the Van Impes have shipped tons of literature, including books, tracts, and magazines, as well as sermon tapes and videos, all over the world. Currently they supply huge quantities of printed materials to Gospel Revival Ministries, which distributes them in some 80 nations.

Dr. Van Impe's voice continues to reach millions overseas via global radio, utilizing Pan American Radio's vast networks. Also, *Jack Van Impe Presents,* the ministry's half-hour weekly telecast, is seen around the world via various international cable networks.

In addition, the ministry maintains one of the most extensive Christian websites in cyberspace. Entire books, prophetic teachings, salvation information, and audio streaming and video streaming of ministry programs is available 24-hours daily to multiplied millions of people anywhere in the world via the Internet and the World Wide Web. It's estimated that 3 to 5 million will use this program annually.

Letters We Love...
from around the world

BAHAMAS
Your TV program is so very informative, and I really look forward to it.

SLOVAKIA
Thanks so much for the powerful videos you sent me which opened my spiritual eyes. We need and appreciate your ministry.

FRANCE
I watch your program every Tuesday on Christian Channel Europe. I am Dutch, my husband is Swiss-French-Dutch, and we live in the south of France.

GERMANY
I am very much interested in the way you preach on the TV every morning.

DENMARK
We saw your program on European Christian Channel and it was a real blessing to us. Can you please send a free copy of "*First Steps in a New Direction.*"

UNITED KINGDOM
How I enjoy watching your world news. Each Tuesday morning I finish work at 10 o'clock, dash home, make my cup of tea and put my television on. I video your program, then I copy it and pass it on.

POLAND
Thank you very much for your small package with leaflets and for the very fine book, *11:59... and Counting!*

GHANA
I truly believe your sermon cassette tapes are blessed by God. I have been spiritually awakened after listening to your messages and have now realized I ought to go witnessing for Jesus.

NEW GUINEA
It is a great blessing and enjoyment to learn and study the Word of God from your ministry. I have been longing to learn of the great prophecies since I became a Christian.

BURMA
I read some of your books from my friend, which he loaned to me. They give me so much help.

NIGERIA
The eight cassettes you sent to us have been a blessing. We had a four-day revival with the cassettes, using two each day. About 76 souls came to the Lord Jesus Christ through your messages on cassette.

MALAWI
Thanks for sending the books. Through *Alcohol, the Beloved Enemy*, there are now 77 true Christians who were formerly drunkards. In all, there are 407 people living true Christian lives through your messages on the printed page. God ministers through you in your books.

Such letters arrive from over 100 nations yearly. Responses come from practically every nation on earth.

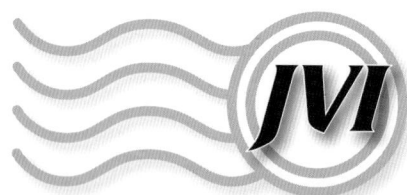

Letters We Love...
from around the world

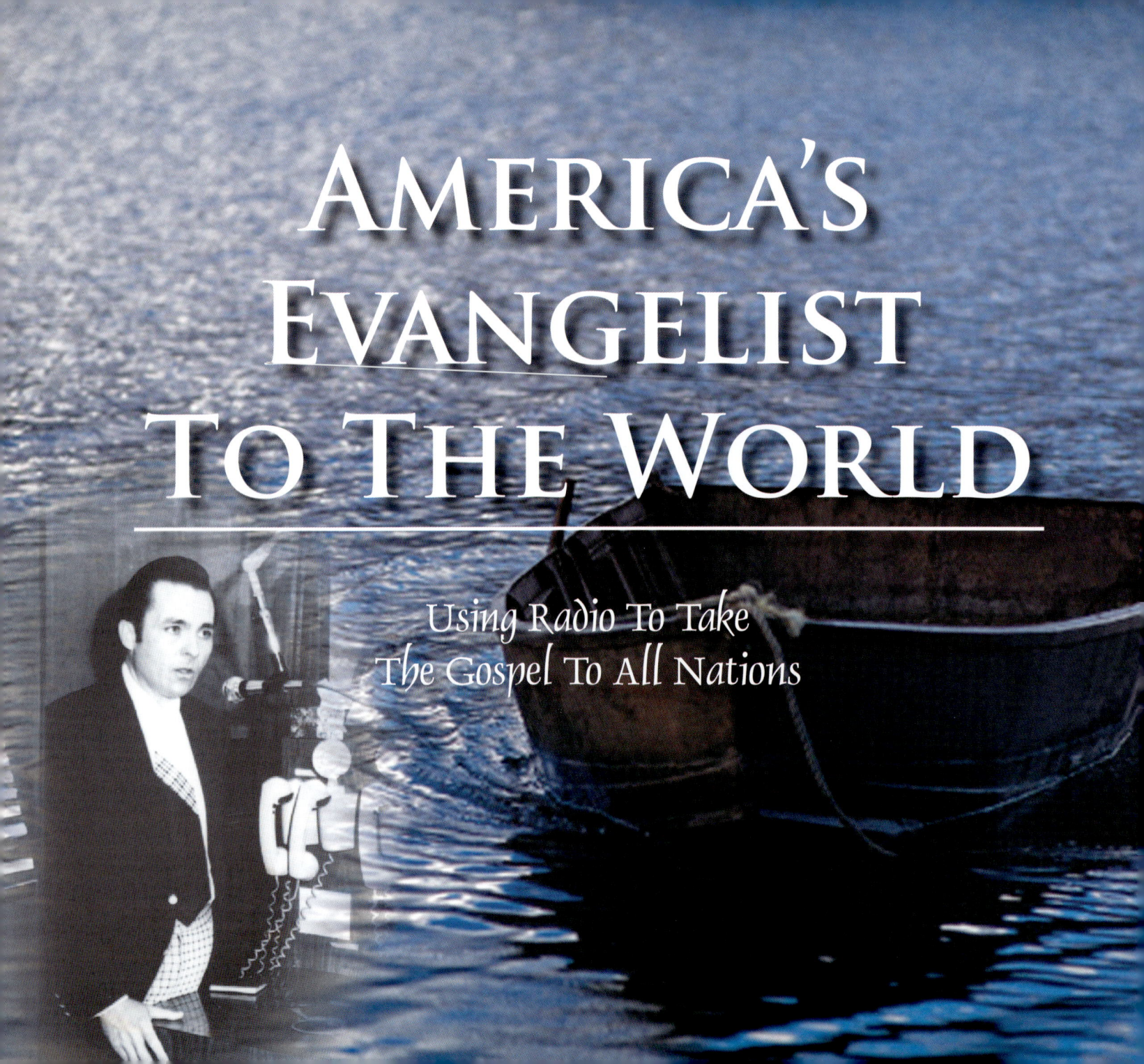

In 1971, Dr. Van Impe began developing a radio program to help reach a greater audience with the gospel. The first effort was to broadcast his recorded sermon, "The Coming War With Russia," on a hundred stations.

Over a period of thirteen weeks, he developed the format for a weekly broadcast. Rev. Charles Ohman, a longtime friend, was the announcer for the program. Rexella was the soloist and shared letters with the listening audience. Dr. Van Impe gave up-to-the minute crusade reports and a Bible message, often on prophetic subjects.

The program was launched on a weekly ongoing basis on Easter Sunday, 1972. It was a major step of faith, perhaps unprecedented in religious broadcasting. Instead of a gradual build-up of stations over a period of months or years, the Van Impe broadcast immediately reached all America via a network of more than 200 stations on the opening day. Within a matter of a few weeks, there began a great and ongoing response from listeners across the nation, some seeking further help, others testifying to being encouraged or led to Christ through the radio ministry.

Less than a year later, the program covered the world! Again the move was made in one great leap, utilizing the global outreach of Trans World Radio. Soon the broadcast was being translated into Russian, Chinese, Spanish, Arabic, and Hebrew, enabling Dr. Van Impe to penetrate areas that were untouchable by conventional missionary means. The broadcast beamed the gospel to literally millions of people worldwide.

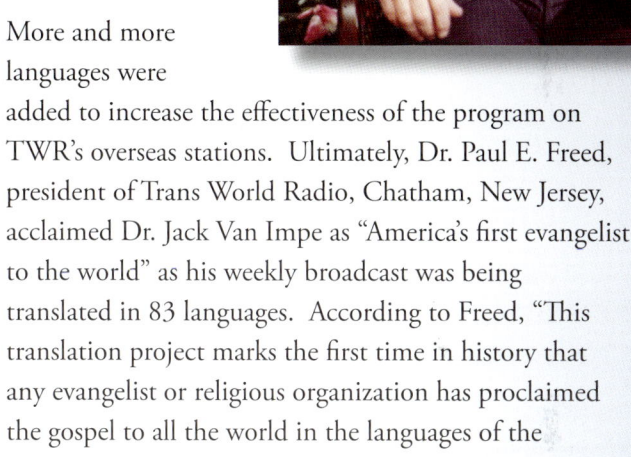

More and more languages were added to increase the effectiveness of the program on TWR's overseas stations. Ultimately, Dr. Paul E. Freed, president of Trans World Radio, Chatham, New Jersey, acclaimed Dr. Jack Van Impe as "America's first evangelist to the world" as his weekly broadcast was being translated in 83 languages. According to Freed, "This translation project marks the first time in history that any evangelist or religious organization has proclaimed the gospel to all the world in the languages of the people."

The outreach of the radio ministry was increased still further when the Van Impe programs were broadcast on the Armed Forces Network, heard around the globe.

Today Pan American Radio broadcasts the Van Impe's message to hungry hearts on every continent of the earth. Listeners from both television and radio in 160 nations have responded to the message of the gospel.

Letters We Love...
about the global radio outreach

CONVERT IN IRAN

I write to express my deepest gratitude for your broadcast which led me to faith in Christ, my Saviour. I am now enjoying the joy which cannot be described.
—*Iran*

REACHING THE UNREACHED

I work at a radio station here in the Philippines where I am broadcasting your program. It is good that people in this region can hear your prophetic insights about current events. I pray that these messages will change and bless thousands of people, and rejoice for the way God is using you to reach the unreached and the untold.
—*J.G.S., Philippines*

SAVED FROM HINDUISM

I am an Asian and a Christian. The Lord Jesus Christ saved me from Hinduism. Your radio program has been a tremendous blessing to me and my family. I have made a new dedication of my life to the Lord and am actively witnessing to my people.
—*D.V.M., South Africa*

RADIO REACHED ME

I am approaching another spiritual birthday. It was through your radio ministry that I became aware of my lost, unsaved condition and asked the Lord Jesus for forgiveness. I am so thrilled that you are on the radio.
—*J.R., Peoria, Illinois*

NEED REVIVAL

Here in this area of Scotland it is hard to find a church that really preaches the gospel. We certainly need a revival. So we especially appreciate and enjoy your radio messages.
—*A & S.D., Montrose, Scotland*

ON-AIR PREACHING LED TO SALVATION

Back in 1977 I tried to find myself in religion. I was not saved and was confused about so many doctrines. I listened to you on the radio on Sunday mornings. I did not go to church because I had to work. Your preaching led to my salvation in 1978. God bless you.
—*R.P., Disney, Oklahoma*

COMPELLED TO LISTEN

As I tuned in Radio Paradise, I heard one of the most powerful, challenging, soul-stirring messages. I was about to work in my garden but I was compelled to sit and listen to the entire message. Thank God for preachers like you.
—*G.C., Nevis Island, West Indies*

EGYPTIAN FINDS PEACE WITH GOD

Your broadcast led me to peace with God. Your voice is heard in every home here in Alexandria, and your admirable programs are much appreciated.
—*Alexandria, Egypt*

Letters We Love...
about the global radio outreach

ENCOURAGED IN IRELAND

How much I enjoy your ministry on Trans World Radio. Your sermons have been a great encouragement and challenge to me. I thank God for your faithfulness to His Word in this day of liberal preaching.

—*K.S., Northern Ireland*

SPIRITUAL THIRST QUENCHER

Thank you very much for your radio program. I have been listening for a while and your inspiring messages are a great blessing to me. They are my spiritual thirst quencher. God bless you as you continue witnessing to the world.

—*H.M., Kenya*

REACHING 332 MILLION AFRICANS

Radio Africa has just ended its most tremendous year of outreach. Through the radio ministries of people like you, we are blanketing English-speaking Nigeria and all of West Africa. Your programs on Radio Africa's 50,000 watt transmitter reach 332 million Africans in 30 countries.

—*Pierce International Communications, Saratoga, CA*

STILL GOING ON FOR THE LORD

I wish to let you know that I listen to your program every Friday and started listening since my conversion in 1981. I thank God that it is only through your program that I am still going on for the Lord.

—*D.A., Papua, New Guinea*

BLESSING IN MALAYSIA

I hear your programme on Trans World Radio and it has been a blessing to me. I thank the Lord for making this possible.

—*S.E.N., Malaysia*

BELGIAN LISTENER BLESSED

Thank you so much for your program on Trans World Radio. One of your recent programs was so special to me. I felt especially blessed when I repeated the prayer at the end of the program. Please send me the booklet, *First Steps In A New Direction*.

—*J.L., Belgium*

Am Not I Better To Thee Than Ten Sons? —*I Samuel 1:8*

From the beginning of their marriage, Jack and Rexella were very much in love and thrilled with their life together. Like most newlyweds, they made great plans for their future. Both of them loved children and talked about having a family of their own someday.

Although Rexella wanted a baby, she was very much aware that she and Jack, living in "borrowed bedrooms" across the nation, did not live a very "normal" life. But after a few years went by and there were no children, she became disturbed.

In her prayer time, she wrestled and bargained with God, promising that if He'd give her a baby, she would continue to travel and support her husband on the road. No answer came.

Then one night as Rexella was begging the Lord for a family, she had a dramatic confrontation. "I heard God's voice as plain as I've ever heard anyone speak to me in my life," she remembers. "He said, 'If you ask one more time, I'll give you a child but it—and you—will be weak.'

"I cried, 'Oh, no, Lord, I'm sorry. Forgive me—I only want Your perfect will. Whether you give me a family or not, I rejoice in what my life is going to be, because it will really be the best for me.'

"That night I became submissive. I had to give my will—to surrender *all*—everything—to Jesus. I've never been sorry. Sure, I've missed not having our own child—there's something in every woman, I think, that cries out to reproduce, to fulfill a maternal desire. But peace came to me.

"Certainly I can relate to the Old Testament story of Hannah, who wept and grieved before the Lord because she did not have children. My dear husband, Jack, said the same words to me as did Hannah's husband—'Am not I better to thee than ten sons?' And he is.

The Van Impes never had children, but God did give them contentment in their relationship with each other…and with Him. Over the years, spiritual children by the tens of thousands have been born through their ministry. Today, Jack and Rexella have a spiritual family that encircles the globe.

Today, Jack and Rexella have a spiritual family that encircles the globe.

Dr. Jack Van Impe, Christian Scholar

Study To Show Thyself Approved Unto God...

Study to show thyself approved unto God, a workman that needeth not to be ashamed, rightly dividing the word of truth.

–2 Timothy 2:15

Few people in modern times have spent as many hours in study as Jack Van Impe. A disciplined and goal-oriented scholar, he was an A student in both high school and college. In addition to school studies, throughout his childhood and well into his half century of ministry, he spent two to three hours each day memorizing music and practicing the accordion.

From Bible college days on, he spent from two to three hours daily memorizing Bible verses—not in chapter order, but by subject, also learning the chapter-verse reference. He now knows and can quote at will, a total of 15,000 verses! His amazing prowess is demonstrated on each weekly telecast as he links dozens of relevant prophetic verses in his commentary on the weeks news reports.

Few realize the rigorous schedule Van Impe maintains to be prepared for his work. Every day he goes through numerous newspapers, magazines, and publications from around the world, reviews scripture passages that relate to current events, and reads from the two or more books he has going at any given time.

Rexella notes that when they travel, Jack always carries a valise filled with books. Even on a week-long trip to speak at a conference, or during a few days of vacation, he may complete 10 books or more. A speed reader, he can devour a 200 page book in a little more than an hour! Van Impe estimates that he has read 11,000 volumes over the past 58 years.

Jack completed his studies and received his degree from Detroit Bible College—now William Tyndale College—in 1951. He immediately plunged into full-time church evangelism, being in crusades up to forty weeks a year.

By 1968, he had conducted several hundred local church crusades and some 60 united, areawide meetings.

In 1968, Jack received a call from one of the most admired and respected pastors in America, Dr. Lee Robertson of Chattanooga, Tennessee. He asked Van Impe to be the commencement speaker at the Tennessee Temple Schools graduation, and informed him that the school would be conferring upon him the Doctor of Divinity degree, along with Rev. Jerry Falwell and Rev. Hugh Pyle

After completing a citywide crusade in Altoona, Pennsylvania, Jack and Rexella drove all night to get home in time to catch a plane for Chattanooga. On the evening of May 27th, Van Impe delivered the commencement address, then was awarded his first doctorate. He also received a deluge of notes, letters, and telegrams of congratulations from friends across the nation who felt that he had well earned his degree through long hours of study and years of faithful service.

Since then, seventeen more Christian colleges and conservative seminaries have bestowed doctorates upon him. Dr. Van Impe is recognized as an extraordinary Bible scholar and one the world's leading experts on Bible prophecy.

A Voice Crying In The Wilderness Of Our Time

Prime Time Television!

In 1975, during the Indianapolis crusade, Dr. and Mrs. Van Impe videotaped their first one-hour television special to be broadcast in prime time. Because of his deep knowledge of Bible prophecy and the widespread interest in this topic, the first special was on "The Second Coming."

The response to this telecast was almost overwhelming, with multiplied thousands of people writing for prayer and requesting information about how to accept Christ. It was immediately obvious that the Van Impes had developed a tremendously effective evangelistic outreach.

So they produced more. In 1976, they produced a show with a bicentennial theme from a tense and troubled Philadelphia. Others followed, from Buffalo, New York; Greensboro, North Carolina; Alaska, Hawaii, and the nation's capital, Washington, D.C.

Each special attracted a sweeping national audience and a harvest of souls and spiritual decisions. The ratings indicated viewing audiences in the millions, which meant that Dr. Van Impe was preaching to more people in a single night via television than he had reached in a lifetime of crusade services.

Over the next few years, the Van Impes produced a total of 19 major prime-time specials at a pace of about three per year. Topics ranged from basic evangelistic themes, to the Christmas story, to prophecy, to more controversial issues, such as "The Occult World," "Escape the Second Death," "Armageddon," and "The AIDS Cover-Up." The TV cameras also traveled to London, England, and to Israel to produce on location telecasts.

The quality of the program's content and production values attracted the attention of the respected Religion in Media organization, which presented Jack Van Impe Ministries with its prestigious "Angel" award for excellence in media presentation. The "Angel" is equivalent to the secular television industry's "Emmy" award. Over the years, Van Impe productions have received 33 silver "Angel" awards, and both Jack and Rexella have been honored with "Golden Angel" awards for lifetime achievement.

How effective were the prime time television specials in reaching people for Christ? Only eternity will reveal the full record. But the ministry received 60,000 requests for prayer and Christian literature from one single prime-time program! Phone and mail records reveal that tens of thousands of souls were reached annually, and there are converts from Van Impe TV programs in more than 6,000 churches across the nation.

Dr. and Mrs. Jack Van Impe produced 19 hour-long prime time television specials which aired on hundreds of stations across North America, reaching multiplied millions of homes. Up to 60,000 people responded to one single TV special, requesting prayer and Christian literature. Follow-up helped place converts in more than 6,000 churches across the nation.

Letters We Love...
about the national television specials

DAYS OF SINNING OVER

I saw your show in Philadelphia and prayed with you. I have not been in church for 20 years, but what you said made a lot of sense to me. After I prayed I couldn't understand how I could feel so good all of a sudden. I am one of the big sinners you spoke about, but after praying, I believe my days of sinning are over.
—W.K., Linwood, Pennsylvania

HUSBAND SAVED THROUGH TELECAST

It was hearing Rexella's beautiful music and the interviews, and Dr. Van Impe speak on prophecy that made my husband realize he was lost and that he did not want to go to hell. God bless you both.
—L.S., Yakima, Washington

SPECIAL MOVED ME TO TEARS

I watched your special tonight, and to say the least, you moved me like an earthquake moves the earth! I repeated the prayer after you and asked God to come into my life and forgive my sins. While I was watching your show I came to tears many times out of love, pain, fear, and guilt.
—G.M., Helena, Montana

FREE FROM THE DEVIL

I've just watched your program on TV. I had been praying for an answer to my confused mind. I have messed with witchcraft and the occult, and I had a bad car accident. Ever since then I've been afraid I'd gone too far. But now, thanks to you, I know better. I'm now a born-again Christian and I'm free from the devil.
—K.P., Denton, North Carolina

TONIGHT WAS A MIRACLE

Your TV program was a great blessing. Your wife's marvelous singing and your powerful, spirit-filled sermon helped me to accept Jesus. I sought for a year and tonight was a miracle night in my life. I served as an elder in the Jehovah's Witness movement for 25 years. I can no longer accept their false theology. Your presentation tonight helped me to learn the truth.
—R.G., Peoria, Illinois

TV SPECIAL OPENS DOORS

My wife and I were very moved as we watched your show. We are but simple folk, and until last night we were distraught, miserable, lost. But we prayed with you and both feel doors have been opened to us. Thank you very much for what you have shared with us and millions of others.
—J.L., Montesano, Washington

Letters We Love...
about the national television specials

TV MESSAGE HITS HOME

I respect you and your knowledge of the Bible very much. You preach the Word with such authority. It was through seeing one of your TV Specials in 1979 that the impact of Christ's Second Coming hit me and I got saved.

—B.L., Miami, Florida

YOU GAVE ME HOPE

I watched your show on April 2 with my wife. We were in Memphis, Tennessee, in a motel room awaiting an operation on our blind son. The TV happened to be on when your show came on the air. You gave me hope, courage, and strength. I watched it with tears and am still weeping as I write this letter.

—S.S., Rupert, West Virginia

AIDS PATIENT WANTS CHRIST

I have been diagnosed with AIDS. I need desperate help to get this demon off my back. I'm also having great difficulty putting cigarettes out of my life. I saw your program this evening and appreciate all that I heard. I said the prayer along with you and truly want the true Christ in my heart.

—D.D., San Francisco, California

YOU HELPED ME BE SAVED

Your ministry had a part in my salvation when I was an alcoholic and drug addict. I watched your program and prayed with you. I am one sheep that the Great Shepherd might not have had if you hadn't been obedient to His call.

—L., Charleston, West Virginia

I FEEL DIFFERENT

I prayed the prayer with you at the end of your telecast, and I feel like a different person. I'm going to start back to church and start taking my three children.

—S.F., Claremore, Oregon

SUICIDE STOPPED

Your TV special was very inspiring to my spirit. My life was full of tears and turmoil. I was addicted to marijuana. I was going to commit suicide with a .25-automatic, but the Lord knocked hard on my door and I finally opened it. Thank you for sharing your TV special.

—V.P., San Angelo, Texas

A Flame of Hope, Light, and Power...

I have known Jack Van Impe since he was a very young man, just out of college, and I've been at his side throughout most of his ministry. I've seen the most intimate part of his personal life, and watched him at work in every aspect of his ministry, fulfilling the divine calling that so obviously rests upon him.

Even in the beginning I was amazed at his preaching. He was so passionate about his message, so forceful, so authoritative. He knew what the Bible said…and what it meant. And He hammered those truths home, clearly and dramatically.

When we began our married life together as traveling evangelists, with no sponsors, no guaranteed income, and no confirmed schedule, he helped me learn to trust God to provide for all our needs. Even with no home of our own, living out of suitcases in borrowed bedrooms, I felt safe and secure with him. His practical faith and deep trust in God inspired confidence in me.

While I've always recognized Jack's brilliant mind and his incredible spiritual insight into God's Word, I also understand far better than anyone else ever could the dedication and self discipline that has constantly driven him to prepare for greatness.

As a young bride, I was amazed at the direction and sense of purpose I saw in Jack. And I felt awesome admiration as I saw him spend two to three hours every day consuming, devouring, and memorizing the Bible. He never missed a day, feeling a direct accountability to the Lord.

While he never set out to become known as "The Walking Bible," memorizing more than 15,000 verses by topic and reference has such a transforming influence on his ministry that it is immediately evident to all. From the beginning Jack was keenly aware that God had something special for us to do. He told me this when it was just the two of us speaking in countless small churches across America.

Jack's growing knowledge and understanding of the Bible made him a trailblazer in many areas. Early on he started preaching profound prophetic messages, explaining the complex passages from the Old Testament and the Book of Revelation. He talked about the vital role of Russia in endtime events before anyone else I knew did. Here was a young man in his 20s saying that we were going to see…*what we are seeing today!*

My husband's favorite Bible verse is Romans 1:16 — **For I am not ashamed of the gospel of Christ: for it is the power of God unto salvation to every one that believeth.**

That was—and is—his drive. He is not ashamed of the gospel. Because he believes the Word of God has answers for all of life's questions, he is willing to take a stand even on controversial subjects that often bring criticism and opposition.

Proclaiming the Truth of Christ's Revelation —By Rexella Van Impe

This stand upon the Word has also helped him live the pure life he has always preached. He has practiced the standards of the Bible so he could say with Daniel, "I purpose in my heart that I will not defile myself" (see Daniel 1:8). Jack has always tried to live as an example of the believer. And as a result, knowing him from a closer perspective than anyone on earth, I've never had to be embarrassed by his life. And the seeds of respect I had for him in the beginning days of our courtship have only grown.

Nobody will ever understand how much it cost my husband to spend some forty years on the road as an itinerant evangelist. More than anyone I've ever known, he loves to be home. I remember once when we getting ready to leave for a three-month crusade tour, Jack stood at the door, dreading to leave home so much that he cried. He often told me that he could never stand to go into an empty hotel room if I were not there with him.

But although I look at Jack Van Impe as my partner, my friend, and my husband, I also see him as a messenger of God, a true hero of the faith. I've always respected him as a minister.

But something strange and wonderful happened one evening as I watched my husband step into the pulpit. As he quoted his text and began to speak, the anointing and presence of the Lord flowed through him in such a forceful, dramatic way that it was absolutely overwhelming. People all over the auditorium were sensing the same impact I was feeling.

I looked up…but I didn't see the familiar figure of my husband. Instead I saw an intensely bright light—like a fire. I saw a flame of hope, light, and power…and heard a thunderous voice proclaiming the Truth of Christ's Revelation. It was breath-taking, awe-inspiring.

I will never forget that momentous night. And I have never been quite the same since. I am so keenly aware that now, more than any other time in all of human history, people need to hear the Word of God and to prepare for the things prophesied for these last days.

Without sounding melodramatic, I believe with all my heart that God has raised up Jack Van Impe to be a "voice crying in the wilderness" of our time, preparing for the coming of the Lord!

Souls Unlimited!

BRINGING THE LOST TO CHRIST

Jack Van Impe started his evangelistic ministry with a crusade in the small town of Filion, Michigan. His first large united crusade was in the same vicinity. Eleven denominations took part in sponsoring the meetings and the press gave glowing reports of the public response.

The president of the sponsoring association called the crusade "two weeks of the most wonderful interdenominational evangelistic meetings Huron County has ever known." In a published report, he went on to say:

> *Hundreds listened attentively every night to the forceful, dynamic Bible truth preached by Rev. Jack Van Impe, and to the beautiful hymns sung by his wife, Rexella.*
>
> *The whole county is stirred, and many who had never thought of doing it before are now leading others to Christ. Many congregations are reporting that their pastors are preaching with a new zeal and passion for souls. Some are reporting an increase in attendance at their Sunday evening services.*
>
> *Many have asked forgiveness and wrongs have been made right. Several pastors have stated that this is the closest thing to old-time revival they have seen.*

THE PATTERN OF SUCCESS

The write-up for that crusade might well have served as the report for more than 260 united efforts to follow. The pattern everywhere was packed auditoriums with overflow crowds, hundreds of decisions, and a surge of spiritual refreshment.

The cooperating churches helped promote the crusades and provided volunteers to serve as ushers, personal workers, and mass choir singers. The hundreds of converts in each service were referred to the sponsoring local churches, who followed up those making decisions for Christ to provide further encouragement and counsel.

The Jamestown, New York, crusade was described by the sponsoring committee as "the most successful meetings in the history of our united efforts." The reporter noted, "Perhaps the greatest evidence of the work of the Holy Spirit was seen in the fact that literally hundreds of Christians flooded the altar and aisles on two different occasions giving their lives in new dedication to Christ."

The Benton Harbor, Michigan, crusade news story described the final service as "the largest crowd ever to assemble for a religious meeting" in that area.

By 1969, the Van Impes had conducted 65 united crusades, and invitations for meetings were coming so fast that there were 1,500 churches on their waiting list.

Rexella recalls her husband showing her invitations from 20 churches in one area, and in another city, requests from seven churches wanting meetings. It was obvious that they must minister exclusively in united, area-wide meetings.

With the move to areawide crusades, Jack and Rexella realized they could no longer stay out on the field ministering and handle the organizational and business details from a motel room. They added an advance man to help arrange dates, places, and details with the crusade sponsoring committees. Rev. Sam Woolcock was their first team member. He served the Van Impe ministry for more than six years, organizing over 100 large crusades.

GOD AT WORK

Many people noted the evidence of the hand of God at work through the expanding ministry of Jack and Rexella Van Impe. There were numerous incidents that obviously were not arranged or contrived by man.

During a large crusade in New York, a liberal minister attended one night and mocked the evangelist throughout his entire message on the cross. Van Impe warned him from the pulpit that God would deal with such disrespect.

A few weeks later, while the unrepentant pastor was speaking on Sunday morning, the church steeple crashed through the roof of his church, landing at his feet. No one was injured, but the city condemned the building and the people did not have the money to rebuild. The event ended the mocker's ministry and closed the church.

An 80-year-old woman wrote to the Van Impes about coming to Spartanburg, South Carolina for a meeting. Although she had no experience in crusade set-up, she insisted that she would contract the auditorium and personally contact all the pastors to insure their cooperation and participation.

While the prospect of the meeting at first seemed a bit far fetched, there was no way to slow down or say no to "Ma" Murray. So the crusade went on, and produced the largest crowd ever assembled for a religious meeting in Spartanburg.

In Pontiac, Michigan, Rexella's home town, the Van Impe crusade was held in a large outdoor stadium. On the final night, threatening rain made them consider moving the meeting to a church auditorium, which would have reduced the space and the attendance dramatically. So they decided to stay outdoors. It rained all day, finally stopping at 7:10 p.m. At 8:00 p.m. it started to sprinkle.

Immediately Dr. Van Impe and the entire congregation joined in praying that the rain would stop. The rain increased to a downpour, with the exception of one city block. The news release the next day reported the event as a 20th century miracle.

Earnestly, Tenderly, Jesus Is Calling, "Oh, Sinner, Come Home!"

THE IMPACT OF AREAWIDE CRUSADES

The crusades continued to break attendance records and to leave spiritual revival in their wake.

In Indianapolis, Indiana, 12,000 gathered for the closing service of the crusade. Hundreds were converted. A cold week for outdoor meetings, thousands gathered nightly wrapped in blankets to hear "The Walking Bible."

Over 10,000 attended the final night in Dayton, Ohio. The huge indoor stadium was packed, night after night. It was a week of great spiritual victories with many decisions for Christ.

"Crusade Crowds Larger Than Any Sports Gathering in the History of Hershey, PA" was the headline on the *Newsletter* report of that meeting. The attendance set a record for any religious gathering in that part of the state.

Portsmouth, Virginia, produced such crowds that closed-circuit TV was used to accommodate the overflow. There were 600 conversions.

The results of the Honolulu, Hawaii crusade in 1974 were exceptional. Thousands attended the meetings in the Waikiki Shell and there were more than 500 conversions. Jack Van Impe appeared on radio with AKU, the highest-paid radio personality in the world and was given the opportunity to answer Bible questions for listeners.

All together, the Van Impes conducted more than 270 mass areawide crusades (plus 800 single church crusades for a total of 1,070 crusades) which attracted a combined audience of some ten million people. Some 600,000 came forward in crusade altar calls to receive Christ as Savior.

...He Shall Give His Angels Charge Over Thee, to Keep Thee in

In 1979, the Van Impes took a vacation trip to Belgium to visit Jack's relatives. The trip was a gift from friends in honor of the couple's wedding anniversary.

Toward the end of their week-long visit, Jack and Rexella drove to Brussels for an afternoon of shopping. After walking and browsing through various shops, they stopped for afternoon tea. Laughing and talking together, they recalled events from their years together, praising the Lord for His faithfulness and goodness.

Later, driving back to the home of one of Jack's cousins to get ready for a family dinner, disaster struck suddenly. From out of nowhere, a bus traveling 50 miles per hour smashed into the Van Impe's borrowed car. The passenger side of the car was ripped away and the rest of the vehicle completely demolished.

Rexella remembers crying out, "Jack, there's a bus!" He attempted to swerve away but it was too late. There was a crunching impact, and her body was hurled out of the car into the busy street. Her last thought as she crashed onto the pavement was, *So this is what it's like to die!*

In a magazine article about the event, Rexella wrote: "I wish in some way I could convey the peace that I experienced from God at that moment. Even Christians sometimes wonder, and perhaps are afraid of the unknown—that valley of death through which we all must pass someday. I would love to stand on a mountaintop and shout to every believer everywhere, 'Don't be afraid.' I can say from experience that at the moment of departure, He is there to give us peace and sustain our hearts. He will never allow us to go through the transition from this life to the next in fear.

"Everything was black! I felt no pain until the warm tears of my sweetheart falling on my face revived me. His voice was choked with emotion as he prayed. I felt myself slipping away from him and I wanted him to know how much I loved him. 'Honey, I think I'm dying…I don't want to leave you!'

"'Oh, no,' he said. 'Oh, God, please help us. Somehow spare her life!'

"Then, again out of nowhere, a hand grasped my wrist and a man stood beside me. He tenderly placed a blanket over my body, and, in perfect English, said, 'Don't move her. She's going to be all right.' As he spoke, my mind became clear and I felt a great assurance and peace that I was going to live."

As quickly as the man had appeared, he was gone. No one ever knew who he was, where he came from, or where he went. The Lord had sent this man—or angel, only He knows—to provide perfect comfort and to minister to the stricken couple. ***Are [angels] not… ministering spirits, sent forth to minister for them who shall be heirs of salvation?*** (Hebrews 1:14).

All Thy Ways

Rexella was taken to a hospital, where x rays revealed that she had a broken collarbone and two broken ribs—one almost puncturing her lung. She had also sustained numerous cuts and bruises. For the next four hours doctors cleaned fragments of glass from her legs, head, and ears. Miraculously, her face and eyes escaped any damage. Because of her undiagnosed head injury, doctors could not give her any pain medication for 18 hours.

Jack spent the next 48 hours getting Rexella released from the hospital and arranging ambulance and wheelchair service from the airline. The trip home was long and arduous, and Rexella managed to withstand the trip by claiming the promise of 2 Timothy 4:17–
Notwithstanding the Lord stood with me, and strengthened me.

In a letter to ministry supporters, Jack expressed his thoughts about the accident: "As the bus hit us, I felt that our earthly life was ending, and we would momentarily be in the presence of the Lord. I was at peace…

"I also realize anew that material possessions are not important. Had Rexella and I not regained consciousness, we would have left all our earthly possessions behind. Only our service for Christ would have accompanied us through the heavenly portals. I have quoted the following verse so often, and now realize the meaning of it more than ever—

> ***Only one life, 'twill soon be past,***
> ***Only what's done for Christ will last.***

Letters We Love...
about the areawide crusades

THANK YOU FOR BEING THERE

You may not recall a hot, humid, miserable night in July of 1973—but I will never forget it. It was on that shirt-sticking-to-your-back night that you held a meeting in the auditorium of Findlay High School. Seated about two-thirds of the way back from the front of the auditorium was a young couple, recently married, the lovely young wife expecting a child.

The young husband was already the kind of guy who had all the answers, believed in himself and, in general, reflected all the usual humanist routines.

This young couple had been "dragged" to hear this "Van Impe guy" by older, well-meaning neighbors. After some rather strange-sounding songs, the main event came on! The exact words that were spoken that night are no longer remembered. What *is* remembered with clarity is the weight on the chest of this young dude. The burden grew greater as you continued to speak. It seemed that every eye in the room was staring at this one young couple! How could all of these people know of their sin?

While others went forward to the altar at the end of the evening, this particular couple remained seated. A strange feeling had come over the guy—a feeling of absolute helplessness. He had NEVER felt like this before. After all, he had always been the one who could handle everything! But not this! This was TOO BIG…SO COMPLEX…TOO FINAL.

With a lump the size of Mount Rushmore in his throat and hot tears of shame coursing down his face—even dampening his mustache—the young Know-It-All gave his heart to the Lord that hot summer night in 1973. Unknown to him, his lovely young wife had rededicated her life to the Lord at the same time.

It was a quiet ride back to Bluffton. The older neighbors listened as the young couple quietly spoke about what had happened to them. The neighbors helped them find a church family and even started a neighborhood Bible study that summer to help the "babes" grow up. (Funny—my wife and I are now the age of that "older" couple!)

We attend a strong Christ-centered church, and both of our businesses are flourishing (after committing them to Jesus).

That "baby" who attended your service while yet unborn has been joined by two sisters and a brother. All have given their hearts to the Lord.

Thank you for being there, Brother Jack! I thank God that the Holy Spirit put all three of us there to hear you that night so long ago.

In *agape* love,
James E. Hopkins

P.S. We still have "Marked for Death"—the sermon you preached—in our record rack!

Letters We Love...
about the areawide crusades

YOUR SERMON WAS JUST FOR ME

Thanks for having a crusade in Youngstown, Ohio. I cam forward the night of April 8, 1988. I am really living for the Lord now the way I should be. I shudder to think of the horrid example of a "supposed" Christian I set. I was out drinking, swearing, watching women, cutting people down, and generally living a "devilish" lifestyle.

One night after drinking pretty heavily, I lost control of my car and narrowly escaped death. Later, as a bunch of my friends and I got drunk one night, I kept thinking, *Why are we destroying ourselves like this?* I knew I had to make a decision about my beliefs…and my life.

When I heard your crusade was coming, I determined to go. When I told a Christian co-worker about the meeting, he said, "Go for it!" That's exactly what I did. I was the first or second person up front in the altar call.

The next day at work my co-worker took one look at me and could tell I was a changed person. I told him that it was as if I were the only one in the audience that night—that your sermon was just for me! It was truly beautiful how the Lord worked through you to help save and change my life.

—*Bill Davis, Ohio*

SISTER PERSUADED ME TO ATTEND

When you spoke at the Centennial Hall at the University of Toledo, my sister kept after me to go with her. I did go, and what you said was instrumental in my salvation and eventually that of my entire family. I appreciate your ministry.

—*D. B., Ohio*

PASTOR SHARES GOOD REPORT

I was greatly influenced by you in 1970-1971 while working in your crusades in Centerville and Hillsdale, Michigan. A new Christian, I became a counselor at your rallies. I took my cousin and led him to the Lord. He is diligently pastoring a church. I've pastored for several years now and have won hundreds to the Lord. I though you might be interested in some of your fruits.

—*J. S., Augusta, Michigan*

Letters We Love...
about the areawide crusades

WHAT A DIFFERENCE HE MADE IN MY LIFE

I am a full time pastor in Richmond, Virginia, and you had a part in this area of my life. You preached a crusade at the baseball stadium in Hampton, Virginia, in September, 1972, and I came to know Christ. What a difference He has made in my life. Since that time I have graduated from Piedmont Bible College, and my wife and I are serving the Lord. You will never know how grateful I am that you came to Hampton.

—N. P., Richmond, Virginia

SAVED IN A JVI CRUSADE

You are my spiritual father from a meeting you held at Waterford Community Church back in June 1973. Just thought you'd be interested in knowing we're now missionaries to Peru.

—Mr. and Mrs. D. V., Lake Worth, Florida

ONE OF 600,000 SOULS SAVED

With tears in my eyes I am praising God for you and your ministry. I am one of the 600,000 souls that have been saved in your evangelistic meetings. It happened for me in Peoria, Illinois. One day I will rejoice with you in heaven along with the many others who have been saved by Jesus' precious blood.

—P. M., Topeka, Illinois

SON-IN-LAW SAVED THROUGH MINISTRY

Several years ago our son-in-law was killed in an auto accident. He was just 33, and left behind a wife and four children. Before he died, you led him to the Lord. I'll never forget what happened. We just got home from your crusade service one night and my son-in-law looked so miserable. I asked if he wanted to go back to the auditorium and he said "yes." You were still there! You led him to the Lord. I remember you saying you'd never heard a sinner's prayer prayed so sincerely—that you knew his conversion was genuine.

It was really hard for my daughter and the children when he was killed. The man involved in the accident was a drunk driver with a drinking record. But what a consolation to know their husband and father is waiting for them in heaven!

—D. H., Cass City, Michigan

Letters We Love...
about the areawide crusades

Walking Through The Valley Of The Shadow

Any Attacker Would Have To Go Through God's Hand To Get To Us

> "There has been a threat made, but nothing is going to happen. Any attacker would have to go through God's hand to get to us."

During the turbulent times of the late 70s and early 80s, being in the spotlight of major public meetings carried a certain amount of risk.

On Friday night in their Kansas City crusade, Dr. Van Impe was announcing his sermon subjects for the final weekend meetings when he saw a dozen policemen enter the building. One of the officers walked to the platform and handed a note to the chairman of the sponsoring pastors. He came over and whispered in Jack's ear. "The police have discovered a plot to kill you. Keep everybody calm. Officers are watching the crowd and have every exit covered."

So Jack said to the crowd, "You've probably noticed an unusual amount of police in the auditorium tonight. Don't be frightened or alarmed. There has been a threat made, but nothing is going to happen. Any attacker would have to go through God's hand to get to us. So just relax. Rexella's going to come right now and sing for us."

Rexella recalls having to overcome her shock and alarm and focus on ministering to the people. "Somehow the Lord always gives you the strength and composure you need at a time like. I was able to walk out on stage, smile, and say, 'I'm so happy that you're all here tonight.' After the service, people said, 'You were so calm, Rexella, that I wasn't afraid.'"

For the next 48 hours, the Van Impes were not allowed to go anywhere without armed guards. The police discouraged handshaking, Bible signing, and most public contact until the final night of the crusade—and then only with armed officers present. But there was no attack.

It was later confirmed that three men involved in drug trafficking were involved in the plot. A number of "pushers" had been converted in the crusade, disrupting the local narcotics business. The three men decided the troublemaker—Jack Van Impe—had to go. Fortunately their plot was discovered and they did not succeed in their murderous venture.

* * * * *

Hershey, Pennsylvania was another danger spot. The crusade crowds were especially responsive with attendance building to 10,555. Revival was in the air. But there were signs of unrest. A note showed up in the offering that threatened the evangelist's life if he preached the sermon, "A Politician's Greatest Blunder." Men wearing stocking masks showed up in small groups scattered through the auditorium on the night of the announced sermon.

At the motel where the Van Impes stayed, the phone rang with threatening messages throughout the night. Authorities discovered the threats were not coming through the switchboard from outside the motel—the harassing calls were being dialed from other rooms.

It was a trying time, frightening and unnerving. But once again they were kept from harm.

* * * * *

Jack Van Impe was delivered from perhaps the greatest danger of his life during his Bicentennial Crusade in Philadelphia, Pennsylvania, July 4-11, 1976. A well-orchestrated campaign of disruption and violence had been planned for the "city of brotherly love" on America's 200th birthday. These plans were known and recorded in *The Congressional Record,* FBI files, *Reader's Digest,* and in the international English newspaper, *Herald Tribune,* as well as in numerous other publications.

Reporting in his own *Newsletter,* Van Impe said:

"In addition to the published warnings, I had personally received threats in the mail. As Rexella and I stood in our home praying before leaving for Philadelphia, my heart was heavy. I felt that I might not return.

That same morning, my staff had given me a note. It said, 'We are praying that God will bring you back to us safely.' Every staff member had signed it. Being a man, I fought my emotions, but was deeply moved.

"The evening of July 2 was spent in Philadelphia. Three truckloads of militants arrived in front of our hotel and marched past with the clenched-fist salute of the communist movement. On television, radicals were being interviewed. They boldly boasted of the way they would dynamite the city on July 4th.

"The fear could be felt in the air. Millions who had planned to come to Philadelphia stayed away. Downtown hotels that had been booked solid months before were 40 to 50 percent vacant.

"On the opening night of our crusade, 50 of the sponsoring churches stayed away, feeling it best to conduct their own services and avoid any violence. Police filled the city. Six guards were assigned to the crusade platform. My personal bodyguard (who had previously been assigned to the mayor) demanded that I wear a bulletproof vest.

"I tried wearing the vest the first night and felt handicapped. The next day I said, 'Men, I have spent the night in prayer and feel it is a lack of faith to wear this vest for the entire crusade.' From that moment on, perfect peace filled my soul."

Van Impe's peace prevailed, and once again he walked through great peril unharmed.

* * * * *

> *Van Impe's peace prevailed, and once again he walked through great peril unharmed.*

With all their travels to crusades and mission fields, the Van Impes have experienced many harrowing encounters while on the evangelistic trail. There have been countless "near misses" involving automobiles and airplanes as they criss-crossed North America and traveled in 50 countries.

One night, atop a mountain in California, Jack and Rexella found themselves in a blinding blizzard. What first appeared as a gentle snowfall became so fierce they were unable to go on. It was bitter cold and there was no help available. All through the night, Jack kept running the car's engine at brief intervals to keep them from freezing.

To make matters worse, the car kept slowly sliding across the road, closer to the edge of the mountain. They prayed and waited. Finally, in the morning, a truck came and provided assistance. They were able to follow it down the mountain.

On another occasion, in the skies over the jungles of South America, they were in a terrible storm. The plane was being tossed about like a toy. The Van Impes prayed, committing their lives to God. Then, Rexella was able to trust the Lord so completely that she fell asleep on her husband's shoulder.

Yea, though I walk through the valley of the shadow of death, I will fear no evil…(Psalm 23:4).

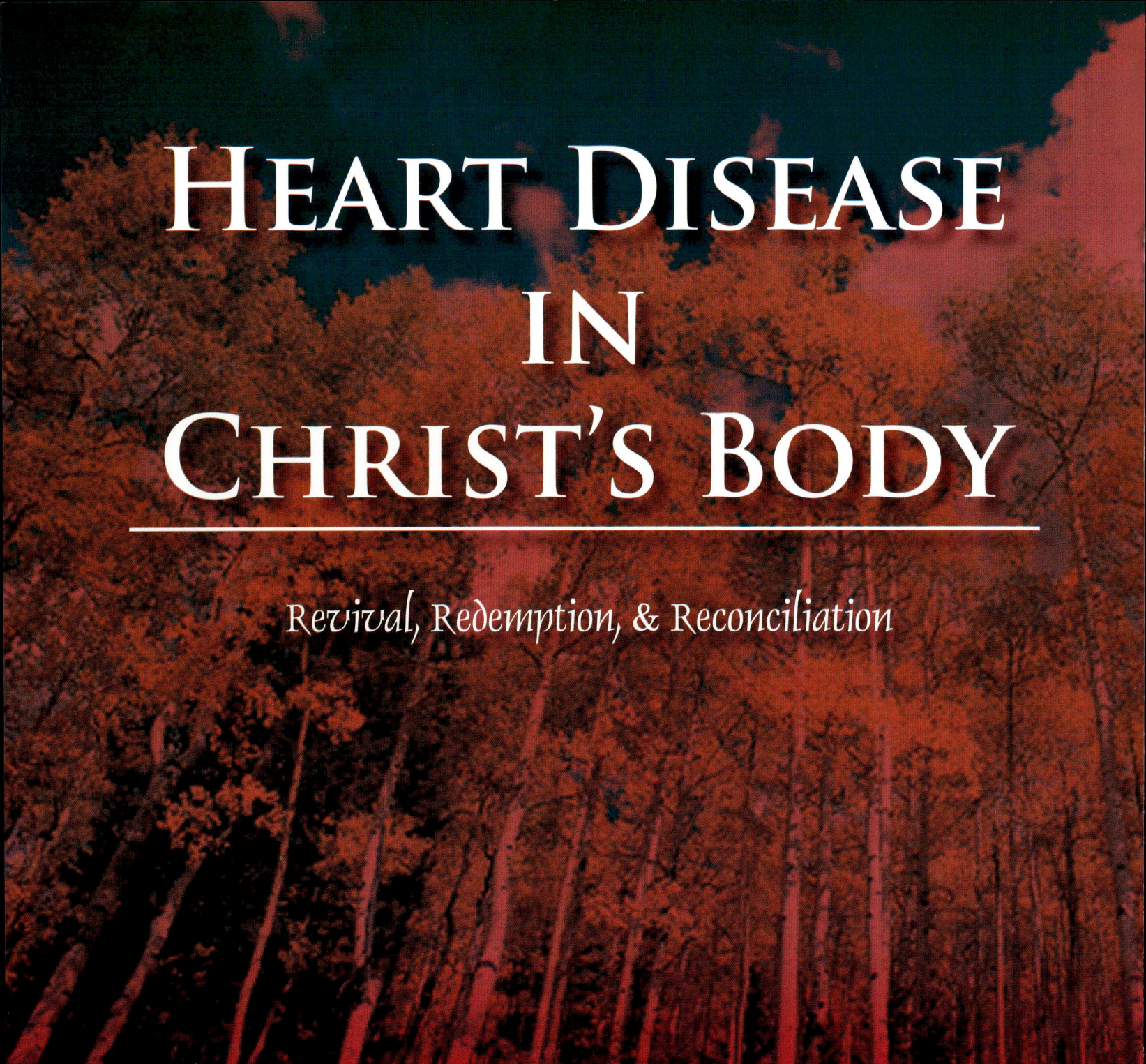

In 1980, the Van Impes discontinued their crusades, after some of the most productive and successful evangelistic meetings in American history. Some ten million people had attended their mass citywide crusades, with 600,000 being saved or restored to Christ.

Why stop such a fruitful harvest? Did the evangelist make a mistake in his decision? *NO, DEFINITELY NOT.*

Jack Van Impe explained his action by saying, "I believe that both **the steps—AND THE STOPS—of a good man are ordered by the Lord** (Psalm 37:23).

Still, such a drastic step was hard for many to understand. Dr. and Mrs. Van Impe began their married life on the evangelistic circuit, conducting revivals in churches across America. They poured our their hearts and lives in ministering and God did a great work in the lives of thousands. New converts were added to the churches in every service, and entire congregations were revived and blessed.

With hundreds more invitations than they could accept, the Van Impes encouraged pastors and churches to cooperate in mass citywide crusades. These large endeavors led to the most exciting and fruitful evangelism in the nation's history. There were huge crowds, tremendous involvement, outstanding results.

Then, at the peak of these spiritual victories and unprecedented ministry accomplishments…God said STOP!

WHY THE CRUSADES WERE DISCONTINUED

For years the Van Impes had been heartbroken at the bickering and contention among church leaders in the planning and scheduling of citywide crusades. As far back as 1966, in Dayton, Ohio, some pastors refused to cooperate because the crusade was being held in the only facility large enough to hold the crowds—the University of Dayton stadium. Because the school was linked to the Catholic church, they refused to support a non-denominational crusade there.

In Durham, North Carolina, there was great animosity and division between various sponsoring churches. One pastor actually said that he was praying for the death of another!

In Sioux City, Iowa, the pastors were openly fighting, and their lack of cooperation had negatively impacted the preparation for and the promotion of the crusade. As a result, on the first night only a handful of people showed up.

Dr. Van Impe called the sponsoring ministers together and said, "This place is almost empty. None of your own church people are even here. If you men don't get together and have this building at least half filled by tomorrow night, I'm going home. I won't be responsible or carry the burden by myself."

Knowing that they had contracted for the auditorium and made other financial obligations, the pastors laid aside their differences and started working. They knew if the crusade was canceled, they'd have to pay the expenses out of their own pockets. The very next night there was a good crowd present. And after a couple of services, the auditorium was jammed to capacity nightly and multitudes came to Christ.

SELF-RIGHTEOUS, HELL-RAISING PHARISEES

By the early seventies, a routine part of the crusade set-up involved having Dr. Van Impe meet with a committee of sponsoring pastors to be "grilled" about his beliefs and practices, about his sermon topics, about who would and would not be welcome as "cooperating" churches. Rather than confirming agreement on basic, fundamental doctrines, the sessions degenerated into petty, hateful, rigid obsessions by so-called "separatists" riding roughshod over all other believers.

It was a shameful and heart-breaking era. Dr. Van Impe recalls that he shared in the offenses. "In my mass, area wide crusades from 1969 to 1980, many good brothers in Christ were barred from participation because I allowed 'militant' leaders in numerous cities to establish false standards of separation. Men who dearly loved God were banned because of denominational tags, or through being classified as 'pseudo-fundamentalists' or 'neo-evangelicals' by the biased views of a vocal minority. Many were deeply hurt. And too often I remained silent."

Dr. Van Impe also remembers that, in addition to concerns over denomination and doctrine, the "super-separatist society" also barred men based on the school they attended or their association with men who had been eliminated from their fellowship. They were also divided over pantsuits, hair-covered ears, and even wire-rimmed glasses!

"Sadly," he said, "those who were so judgmental on these issues were often lenient concerning sexual promiscuity, smutty jokes, and slander within their personal associations and churches. Hypocrisy abounded, and my heart was crushed."

So the announcement was made that the crusades were ended—immediately—with no plans to ever resume. Dr. and Mrs. Van Impe immediately began a weekly telecast to reach out to the people. The programs were prepared in love, and made available to all who wished to tune them in, regardless of their position or "pedigree."

5,000 Christian Leaders Responded...

At the same time he was ministering on TV, Dr. Van Impe was spending hundreds of hours in the Word and in prayer, seeing a scriptural answer to the separatist problem. His in-depth study resulted in a major book, entitled, *Heart Disease in Christ's Body* (now called, *Sabotaging the World Church*).

Invited to speak to the National Religious Broadcasters convention in Washington, DC (on the same night that President Ronald Reagan addressed the delegates), Dr. Van Impe issued a clarion call for unity, love, and reconciliation between the battered and bruised segments of the body of Christ. He received a tremendous ovation from the assembled Christian leaders following his message.

The book, *Heart Disease in Christ's Body,* became an immediate best seller. Copies of the book went to church leaders across North America and circulated in 50 nations overseas. It was distributed to students in Bible schools and seminaries (even being made required reading in some). As expected, the book was controversial, producing outcries of protest from some circles, but also a broad, rising, swelling flood of response from men and women around the world who recognized the desperate need for a return to New Testament Christianity based on Christ's love.

Determined to go it alone, if necessary, and be the lone voice speaking out for true Christian unity and fellowship with all of God's people, Dr. Van Impe was gratified and elated at the overwhelming response from literally thousands of people who said they had been praying and waiting for someone to take a stand and bring change and reconciliation to Christ's body.

Five thousand Christian leaders wrote to tell him how his message had touched and changed their hearts, minds, and attitudes!

...to Jack Van Impe's Impassioned Call to Unity

Letters We Love...
responses to Heart Disease book

MESSAGE MUCH NEEDED

Jack Van Impe's clear desire for spiritual unity in the body of Christ is a great encouragement to me and to many, many others who feel the same burden, expressed by our Lord (John 17:21).
—*Dr. Bill Bright, Campus Crusade for Christ International*

SPIRIT ON EVERY PAGE

Thank you for *Heart Disease in Christ's Body*. It is a masterpiece. The print of the Holy Spirit is upon every page.
—*Dr. M.M., South Fulton, Tennessee*

BACK ON TARGET

You have said what I wanted to say for years. Finally an honest statement about what has happened in fundamentalist circles. I pray that God will use your book to get us back on target.
—*Rev. G.H., Pineville, Pennsylvania*

Letters We Love...
responses to Heart Disease book

SPIRITUAL POLITICS

The revelations of your book made me heartsick. I also have been slandered for not playing spiritual politics with certain religious leaders.

—Rev. W.W., Brown City, Michigan

BOOK MEANINGFUL

You will never know until you get to heaven what this book has meant to my wife and me.

—Rev. U.M., Rutland, Maine

I PREACHED IT

I preached *Heart Disease* Sunday to my congregation. Now I, too, am free.

—Rev. L.T., Hueytown, Alabama

DESTROYING FROM WITHIN

Thank you for addressing the seriousness of our error… I wholeheartedly agree and trust that God will open the hearts of men who are guilty of destroying the Body from within.

—Rev. J.P., Huntingdon, Pennsylvania

BONDAGE OF BIGOTRY

Thanks for having the courage to write the truth. Never again will I be in bondage to the bigotry that formerly enslaved me. Your stand was biblical and I know you took it in obedience to the call of Jesus Christ.

—Rev. S.P., Lancaster, California

ENGLISH PASTOR WRITES

Here in the United Kingdom the same kind of spirit often raises its ugly head. I now am able to grasp more of the situation because of your book.

—Rev. R.A., Kent, England

BEEN BADLY WOUNDED

Your book helped me so much because I have been badly wounded in the church. Only Christ could sustain me. You will never know the good your book has done.

—C.D., Camden, New Jersey

A More Sure Word of Prophecy –2 Peter 1:19

From the time of his conversion at age 12, Jack Van Impe had a healthy curiosity about prophetic matters, with a marked interest in sermons or written material about the subject.

A few years later when he began memorizing Bible verses, that interest burgeoned into a passionate desire for knowledge and understanding. Since so much of the Bible is related to prophetic events, it was inevitable that one memorizing such great amounts of scripture would take a special interest in the signs of the times.

Being an avid reader and a tireless researcher, Jack saw both past and present-day events fitting perfectly into the prophetic outline of the ages. And seeing that past biblical prophecies had been fulfilled to the letter, he concluded that the remaining prophecies were sure to come to pass. These truths found their way into his preaching, even as a young evangelist.

Rexella recalls that early on Jack was preaching profound prophetic messages, explaining complex Old Testament passages and explaining the mysteries of the Book of Revelation. "He loved to explore the new nation of Israel's prominent role in end-time prophecy," she said, "and he talked about the vital role of Russia in that day long before anyone else I knew."

Over the years, Van Impe's emphasis on prophecy struck a responsive chord in the hearts of thousands. Prophecy night in the crusades was often the best attended service of the week. Always the evangelist emphasized the imminence of Christ's return and the urgent need for every soul to be prepared to meet God, which was instrumental in prompting a host of seekers to make decisions for Christ.

Dr. Jerry Falwell, commenting on the long career of Jack Van Impe on the crusade trail, said, "I consider Dr. Van Impe one of the most dynamic and powerful preachers in the land today. More than anyone else on the scene in this generation, he has awakened a great interest in prophecy in the hearts of God's people. He has alerted the Christian public to the lateness of the hour and the critical state of the world. He has used this information as a challenge to souls to turn to Christ."

Undeniably, Dr. Van Impe has felt the pulse of his time and as a result has caught the ear of the world. Sermons such as "The Coming War With Russia" and "Shocking Signs of the End of the Age" were successful because they avoided hysterical speculations and crowd-seeking sensationalism. Rather, they were packed with Bible proofs, with documented facts and a scholarly, in-context presentation of all biblical references.

Since then, in the last quarter of a century, he produced a dozen books on prophecy, including the national best-seller, *Israel's Final Holocaust,* and the classic landmark, *Revelation Revealed, Verse by Verse,* regarded as one of the most important prophetic works of our time.

Dr. Van Impe has written hundreds of articles, produced numerous prime time television specials dealing with issues and topics with prophetic impact, and created at least a score of best-selling videos on prophecy themes. Always a popular prophecy convention speaker, for the last decade, he and Rexella have appeared weekly on *Jack Van Impe Presents,* a world news forum examining current events in the light of Bible prophecy.

As a result, in addition to being known as "The Walking Bible," Dr. Van Impe is recognized as one of the nation's foremost authorities on the subject of Bible prophecy. His bold, cogent commentary on international developments such as the growing importance of Israel and the rise of the European Community attracted international interest. "These two events had to happen before we could honestly say, 'These are the end times,'" he declared.

He also addressed issues such as the AIDS epidemic, the surging growth of cultic religions and the occult, the "mark of the beast," aliens, angels, the New Age movement, America in prophecy, the Millennium, and the threatened advent of Armageddon, among others. With Operation Desert Storm against Iraq, there was a renewed interest by millions in end-time prophecies.

The secular media often turned to Dr. Van Impe's extensive Bible knowledge and prophetic expertise to provide resource for stories which appeared in such respected publications as *U. S. News & World Report, Newsweek, Time,* and *The Chicago Tribune* and scores of other newspapers.

Dr. Van Impe says, "Bible prophecy is more relevant and important now than at any time in our whole ministry—than at any time in the history of the world! I have always preached imminence, that Jesus could come at any moment, and I believe that we are in the windup now.

"Gibbon, the author of *The Decline and Fall of the Roman Empire,* after studying the Church fathers of the first three centuries, discovered that the majority of them proclaimed the six-day theory based on 2 Peter 3:8 and that Christ would return early into the 7th day, or by 2018 at the latest.

Van Impe says, "I certainly don't claim to know 'that day and hour,' but it can't be too much longer. We feel God has raised us up to tell the world, 'Jesus is coming soon—PERHAPS TODAY!'"

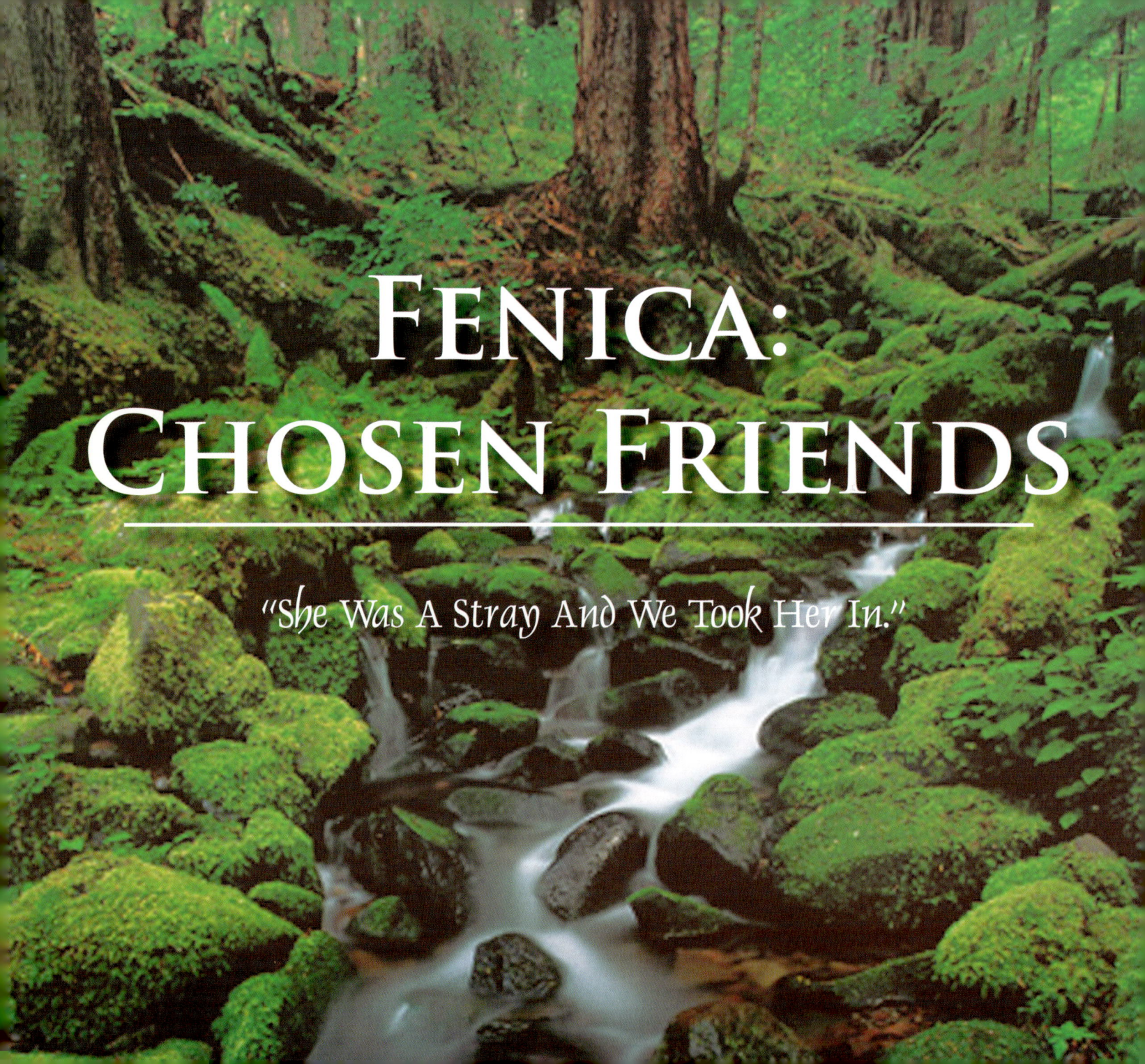

They heard her crying the minute they got out of the car!

The Van Impes had just arrived home from a crusade trip several years ago. It was almost 3:00 o'clock in the morning and they were eager to get the car unpacked and get inside.

But they heard a little cry—almost like the sound of a baby. Rexella hurried over to some nearby shrubbery, reached down…and there was a tiny little kitten. She was so lost, so little, so alone.

Jack discouraged feeding the kitten, knowing that's all it would take for the animal to "adopt" them, and knowing that their travel schedule was not conducive to caring for a pet. But the next morning Rexella talked him into it.

The next step was a trip to the vet for medicine to clear up mites and worms. They made a place for her in the garage and a friend fed the cat for them while they went to the next crusade. Back home again, Rexella wanted to bring the kitten inside. "That's not a very good idea," said Jack. "Oh, just for a little while so I can love her a little bit," Rexella insisted.

The moment she set foot inside the door, Fenica (a derivative of the Belgian word for Josephine—the ending *ca* indicating "precious" or "beloved") became queen of the house. And she never went back to the garage. In two weeks time she went from being an abandoned stray to a member of the family.

FENICA I

WINNING HEARTS

Fenica immediately adapted herself to the Van Impe lifestyle. Because they spent so much time working, she learned independence and self-entertainment. And she took to travel like a real trooper. She began traveling in the car when she was just a month old, always calm, never nervous.

When it came time to fly, she went on the plane with Rexella, and over the years became the veteran of hundreds of flights. She adapted to different hotel rooms without complaint. When Jack and Rexella came in, tired from a busy evening, she'd meet them with a gentle purr, ready to cuddle for a while.

After seventeen years of companionship, Fenica succumbed to a cancerous condition. The Van Impes were greatly saddened by the loss, totally surprised at how much a part of their lives her gentle love had filled.

Fenica had known how to coax Jack into playing games with her on the floor…to snuggle close to Rexella's side when she had her daily prayer time.

After several weeks of painful adjustment, they began praying that God would send them a new kitten, perhaps the same way Fenica had come into their lives. But although they looked outside several mornings, no stray ever showed up. So they decided to go to the humane society shelter.

THE CHOICE

There were only two cats to choose from the day they went looking—one healthy and friendly, with big, curious eyes. The other was a poor, bedraggled ball of gray fur, so weak and sickly it barely opened its eyes. It should have been a simple choice. And it was.

Jack and Rexella chose the poor, sick kitten who so desperately needed help. Either they chose her… or she would die. They both realized the other cat was appealing enough to have a good chance for adoption.

Driving their new pet straight to the veterinarian, they decided her name would be Fenica II, sensing that she had the same trusting nature and gentleness of her namesake. In a matter of weeks the new kitten was the picture of health and had proved to be a sweet, loving animal.

Although some cats have a reputation of being independent and aloof, the Van Impes say that Fenica lives to love. "All we have to do is simply put our hand down and she purrs, then rubs her soft face against our fingers to say, "I'm here." She is sensitive to our every mood and feeling.

FENICA II

TAKING A "LOVE" BREAK

Rexella says, "Jack is a scholar, able to immerse himself into research projects and spend hours engrossed in intense thought. When he's working on a project—desk covered with Bibles, books, clippings, and notes—I've learned to stay away and let him be alone with the Lord.

"But Fenica watches him from across the room for awhile, then goes over and jumps up on his desk. Getting directly in the middle of everything, she stares up at Jack quietly until he takes a moment to notice her.

 "Usually Jack picks her up and gives her a hug and a few strokes, then they "talk" for a bit. I'm always amazed to see how his face softens and relaxes when Fenica comes to whisper in his ear. When he puts her down after a while, he is refreshed, and the cat goes her way, contentedly making the rest of her rounds.

"We also enjoy watching Fenica play with her toys. She throws them in the air and runs to catch them. She rolls and stretches with them, stalks and *pounces* on them triumphantly. Sometimes I'll toss a soft fabric ball to her—her favorite toy—and she bats it back to me with her paw. What fun!

"Jack and I live a very busy life. Producing a weekly television show, heading an international ministry, writing, speaking, making videos, and managing our personal household. You can image how full our schedule is each day. We love it and would have it no other way. But too often I find myself running out of time, having to dress in a hurry to make it to another appointment.

"At my dressing table, putting the last minute touches on my make-up or hair, I'll feel Fenica come sit by my feet, rubbing her soft fur on my leg. She senses that I am about to leave and gently reminds me not to forget to pay her a minute's attention before I go. When I do, it's amazing how her calmness makes me smile, relax, and regain a composure that sends me out better prepared to face my tasks.

"Jack and I are so thankful that God gave us another beautiful, gentle, loving creature to have in our home. Caring for Fenica is a privilege—and we get back so much more than we give. Her presence enhances our life at home a great deal.

"Our care for Fenica reminds me of a beautiful, spiritual comparison. One day Jesus went to the 'pound' of life where we were imprisoned, waiting to die, and He chose us! He redeemed us—then cleaned us up, healed our wounds, nourished our famished souls, and gave us His welcome to abide in His presence! He took us to be His chosen friends, and gave us the privilege…and power…and authority to be productive and useful in the kingdom of God.

"Oh, what a Savior! How could we *not* love Him?"

JACK VAN IMPE PRESENTS...

Reaching More People
In One Night
Than In A Lifetime
of Crusades

January 1, 1980, was the kick-off for a new weekly telecast, "Jack Van Impe Presents." Aired on scores of stations across the U.S. and Canada, the program was not just "another religious TV program," but a unique format designed to communicate the gospel as forcefully as possible.

In addition to Rexella's great inspirational solos and the powerful preaching of Dr. Van Impe, the program featured timely interviews with outstanding guests like Israel's Abba Eban and President Yitzhack Navon, Peter Marshall, Walter Martin, theologian Dr. John Walvoord, Barbara Bush, Chuck Colson, Surgeon General Dr. C. Everett Koop, Colonel Sanders of fried chicken fame, Miss America (Terri Meeuwsen), Miss USA (Terri Utley), and a host of others.

A few weeks later the overwhelming results from the program were evident. Again, the probable viewers for each program nationwide exceeded the number of people reached in all the Van Impe's years of crusades. Responses were coming in at the rate of 1,000 per station per month. The ministry received a total of 60,000 responses in February, and 72,000 during March. The need and hunger of the mass TV audience was awesome.

Over the next five years, as the number of stations carrying the program climbed toward 200, the flow of phone and mail responses created unprecedented demands for literature and spiritual counseling materials by mail. This, of course, required additional staff in the ministry headquarters offices to process the requests.

While spending a full week of each month producing the videotapes for the new telecast, the Van Impes continued their heavy work schedule on the international radio ministry, creating ministry publications, and producing new books and tapes. While willing to "burn out" for the Lord, Dr. and Mrs. Van Impe felt the added strain, especially the added financial burden.

The new weekly TV program was expensive to produce, requiring the use of an outside studio, equipment, and crew, and the ministry had no financial reserves to underwrite the project. So raising funds to cover the cost of the ministry's rapid growth was a necessary and never-ending source of concern.

But after praying and receiving assurance from the Lord that the work of the ministry was worthy and worthwhile in terms of reaching people for Christ, the Van Impes went all out. Their work to harness television to evangelize the nation was heralded by fellow ministers and industry experts alike as innovative and productive.

The reports that really counted, though, came from the viewers who were saved, renewed, encouraged, and informed…from those who wrote to say, *"Your TV program changed my life!"*

Owe No Man Anything!

From the very beginning, Dr. and Mrs. Van Impe regarded television as a ministry outreach tool—an effective means of sharing the gospel, calling the lost to Christ, and reviving and encouraging believers. Both were determined never to use precious airtime begging and pleading for funds.

They had never resorted to such fundraising tactics on radio and felt they should not do so on TV either. They felt that conducting high pressured, impassioned, "emergency" appeals smacked of "commercializing" the gospel, and was not a good testimony to the unsaved and skeptical.

So rather than a money-making income source, the Van Impe TV specials—and even the weekly programs—had to be subsidized from the ministry's general funds. In addition to the additional work of producing the programs, Jack and Rexella had to take on the responsibility of raising the funds for television from crusade offerings and other support from ministry donors through the mail.

"How much did you make on your last national telecast?" Dr. Van Impe was asked by a Pennsylvania TV talk show host.

"Nothing," he answered. "I lost $235,000. And I invite you to come to our headquarters and examine the books. I have nothing to hide." It was no bluff. Had the emcee carried out the investigation, he would have found that viewers contributed only a fraction of the cost of the telecasts. The balance of the funds were donated by churches and individuals who were willing to assist the Van Impes use the power of TV to proclaim the gospel nationwide.

THE GREAT "GIVE-AWAY"

The financial load of paying for production and air time costs for a growing network of stations grew increasingly heavy. To encourage greater response, "expert" consultants advised Dr. Van Impe to offer various gifts on the air—Bibles, books, records, tapes, videos—all for free! They said viewers who requested these free items would respond with ministry support gifts.

Sure enough, response to the telecasts offering various free gifts mushroomed. Working night and day to keep up their crusade ministry, writing responsibilities, and television production schedule, the Van Impes failed to take time to study the ministry's monthly financial statements until they were informed they were facing a deficit!

It was an unbelievable situation. The Van Impes and their entire ministry staff was working at a breakneck pace. The incoming and outgoing mail volume was at an all time high. Everybody was busy! But being busy was not the same as profitable. To their horror, the Van Impes discovered that the ministry was on the verge of bankruptcy!

Because of their policy of never asking the TV audience for funds, giving everything away—the ministry had accumulated a total deficit of some four *million* dollars! How could such a thing happen? An audit showed that out of one million families who requested free books, videos, and other materials, only 35,000 returned so much as a thank you note!

PRACTICING HONOR AND INTEGRITY

Drastic circumstances demanded drastic action! The Van Impes agreed there was only one thing to do—cancel the telecast for a while and find a way to repay the accumulated debt. Although they enjoyed ministering on the air, they were in agreement that the telecasts could not continue.

Dr. Van Impe well remembers the trying times he faced over a four year period in carrying out the Apostle Paul's admonition in Romans 13:8 to **owe no man any thing.** "I always wanted to do what was right," he said. "I was raised in the Belgian tradition of avoiding debt—of paying everything owed at the end of every week if possible. So not being able to pay the suppliers from whom we'd purchased books, tapes, Bibles, and other materials was devastating to me personally.

"I made it a point never to avoid talking to my debtors. So I called everyone to whom I owed money—some 70 to 80 creditors. I said, "If it takes me 'til my dying day, you'll be repaid. It'll take me some time, but each month I'll send you something." They accepted that, and by the help of God, four years later every bill was paid."

How were the funds raised to pay back this crushing deficit? Dr. and Mrs. Van Impe scheduled a grueling tour of partner banquets, night after night in different cities across the nation. Meeting in hotel conference rooms with ministry friends and donors, face to face, the Van Impes sang and played, preached and prayed, and reported the current situation and the long range plans of the ministry. Essentially, the Van Impes asked their friends for a vote of confidence and for financial help to pay off the debt incurred in sharing the gospel freely.

Dr. Van Impe also wrote to all his friends and supporters across the nation and explained the distressing situation the ministry faced. Humbly, without making excuses or blaming others, he took full responsibility for the problem.

Thousands of people rallied to the ministry's support and sent in generous gifts until the indebtedness was paid in full.

Only when the debt was retired did the Van Impes go back on television. They still do not make strong appeals for donations on the air. However, the ministry now charges a reasonable fee to cover the cost of producing books, videos and other ministry materials offered. "After almost having to close our doors," said Van Impe, "we presently ask people to help pay for what they request."

The new policy helps the ministry stay on a sound financial footing, while expanding its telecast to reach the world. And by avoiding urgent financial appeals, the ministry does not offend unsaved viewers or give skeptics cause to doubt.

Declare Ye Among The Nations, PUBLISH...and Conceal Not

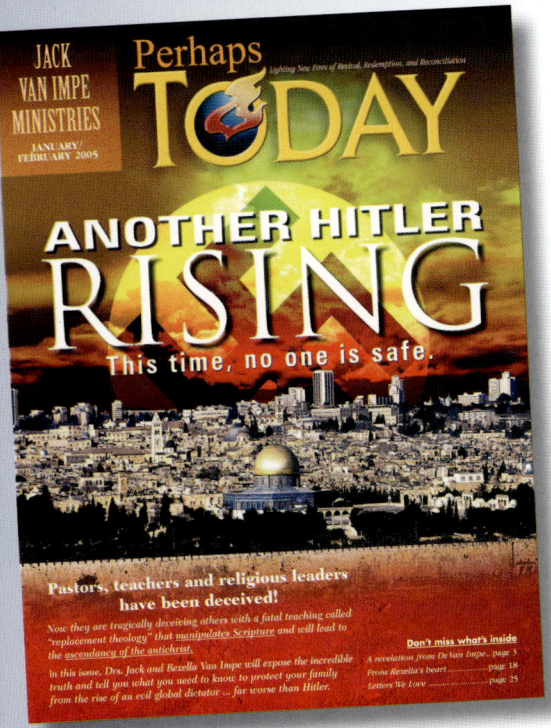

In April, 1969, the first issue of a modest publication titled simply *Newsletter* was sent to friends and supporters of the Jack Van Impe crusade ministry. In addition to providing news updates about the activities of Dr. and Mrs. Van Impe and their itinerary, the publication gave him the opportunity to share new scriptural discoveries and teaching articles.

Dr. Jerry Falwell was of immense help to the Van Impes in that formative time. He and his church, the Thomas Road Baptist Church of Lynchburg, Virginia, produced and mailed their *Newsletter* for the first year at no charge. He also urged people to pray for and support the Van Impe ministry. They will always be grateful.

Year by year the *Newsletter* grew, both in circulation and additional content. In addition to keeping ministry partners and donors informed of the Van Impe's activities, the publication included sermon and teaching articles, ministry reports, and comments from readers.

In 1980, the publication assumed a new name and format, becoming a 32-page digest size magazine, *Perhaps Today*, referring to Dr. Van Impe's strong emphasis on the imminent coming of Christ. The magazine included photos and art in its crusade reports and articles, and also listed the stations across the nation and around the world that carried the Van Impe releases on radio or television.

In the mid-80s, *Perhaps Today* became a full-size, full-color, 24 to 32 page publications, with a circulation exceeding 100,000. Reflecting the Van Impe's commitment to excellence, the magazine dealt with major issues of national and international importance, a strong emphasis on Bible prophesy. In addition to Dr. Van Impe's timely, scholarly articles, there were inspirational reflections from Rexella Van Impe, a forum for letters from readers, a current TV log, and a showcase of attractive and worthwhile books, tapes, and videos produced by the Van Impes and other ministries.

Today the bi-monthly magazine remains one of America's most respected ministry publications, and continues to maintain its reputation for quality, taste, and up-to-the-minute reports on world events in the light of Bible prophecy. The circulation of *Perhaps Today* now reaches 750,000 readers.

– Jeremiah 50:2

In addition to mailing *Perhaps Today* to its active mailing list, the ministry regularly distributed thousands of copies of each issue overseas through various missions channels. The magazine's excellent content, as well as its color and quality made it a popular and sought-after publication. On one occasion, a tribal king in Nigeria included copies of *Perhaps Today* Magazine with the gifts he passed out to guests at his coronation!

Gospel Revival Ministries, under the direction of John Musser, is a very effective missionary organization that continues to distribute Van Impe publications, including magazines and books, into some eighty nations. National pastors and evangelists especially appreciate Dr. Van Impe's material and like to use it in their soul winning projects.

Over the years there has been consistent feedback from ministers and laypeople alike from many countries who either credit the literature to helping them find the Lord, or gratefully report its effectiveness in reaching the lost.

> Dr. Jerry Falwell was of immense help to the Van Impes in that formative time.
> He and his church produced and mailed their Newsletter for the first year at no charge.

Letters We Love...
about publications & literature

MAGAZINE IS BLESSING

I am so happy to receive *Perhaps Today* magazine. The other night I read a recent copy—I read every page before I could lay it down. I always get so much good scripture. I also enjoy Rexella's article—it always does so much for me. I never want you to stop sending the magazines to me.

—A.R., Manchester, Ohio

APPRECIATES MAGAZINE

I really like the news sections you include in the *Perhaps Today* magazine. It is such an inspiration to me and I appreciate it.

—R.B., Cleveland, Georgia

FIFTY SAVED

Thanks very much for the tracts you sent to us. We have used them in our hospital, bus, and prison ministries, and because of them our evangelistic team members have recorded 50 remarkable conversions. To God be the glory!

—E.A., Nigeria

EYE OPENER

Your article, "Don't Let the Devil Sabotage You" in *Perhaps Today* really opened my eyes. I think I matured ten years in Christ by reading it! I intend to save this issue and read it again and again!

—H.D., Traverse City, Michigan

LITERATURE IS BLESSING

The literature you kindly sent me has been a great blessing and has taught me things I might not have ever learned. I am sharing the booklets with other Christians.

—J.M., Dublin, Ireland

JVI BOOKLETS HELP

Your booklets for new converts and the tracts on AIDS was so helpful in our recent crusade. Your material was of great help in counseling the 120 new converts, and I appreciate you support and prayers for the Trinidad meeting. God bless you and your ministry abundantly.

—P.R., Pembroke Pines, Florida

BROUGHT TO CHRIST

I have been touched by your literature. I was brought back to the Lord Jesus through a friend at work who suggested I read some of your material. Thanks so much, and God bless you.

—F.C., Los Angeles, California

LITERATURE MINISTERS IN GUYANA

Thank you so much for the packet of literature and the videotaped message. I share everything you send with my church and to all we can reach. We appreciate your help for we need all the assistance we can get for the Lord's work here in Guyana.

—S.H., Guyana

Letters We Love...
about publications & literature

REACHING AFRICAN PRISONS

I read your tract, "What Must I Do To Be Saved?" while I was in prison. That night I could not sleep—thinking about what I must do to be saved. Finally I prayed for forgiveness of my sins, which was my first prayer in my whole life! God began to move in my life. He changed me and made me a soul winner. There were 32 wardens and 52 prisoners saved. When I was released, I got assigned as preacher in the prison. By God's grace, I now preach in six other prisons. I have established gospel libraries in each of them, and could use more of your literature for this purpose.

—A.R., Ghana

THANK GOD FOR YOU

I knew about God but did not believe in Jesus before. Now, by the help of your *Perhaps Today* magazine and other booklets on salvation, I found Christ as my Saviour. Since then, I have been thanking God for how He so wonderfully used you to save my life. You truly are people of God.

—I.J.B., Nigeria

A NEW UNDERSTANDING

Words could not even begin to express what your ministry has meant to me and my family. Your ministry, literature, books, and tapes have allowed and nurtured a growth in our spiritual lives unlike anything else. A new understanding has grown and developed which I cannot begin to explain.

—A.A., Warren, Michigan

SAVED THROUGH MAGAZINE

I wrote to you a couple of years ago to tell you I was saved by reading your magazine. Thank you for sending it to me. I am Belgian, as you are, on my father's side. I have cousins in Liege, Narnur, Anvers, and a place named Godin. I love Jesus so!

—A.S., Turtletown, Tennessee

JVI LITERATURE WINNING SOULS IN PHILIPPINES

I am very grateful for the books and tracts you sent to use in our ministry here. Praise God, 98 souls have accepted Christ as their personal Saviour and Lord in just three months time, and our church is growing tremendously. Thank you for your contribution to revival in this country.

—Pastor P.S., Nueva Ecija, Philippines

III

Write Thee All The Words That I Have Spoken Unto Thee...

Of all the outreaches that have an ongoing impact and effect on people's lives, Dr. Jack Van Impe's 50 books must play a major role. In addition to being a voracious reader and deep-thinking scholar, he is also a prolific writer, producing an amazing stream of important works throughout his life.

He has written devotional books, collections of sermons, doctrinal studies, and topical books about suffering, child rearing, family living, and alcohol and the Bible. He has written about salvation, holiness, fundamentalism, the Holy Spirit, as well as books on prophetic topics, several of which have been best-sellers and are now regarded as classics.

Considered one of America's foremost authorities on Bible prophecy, Van Impe has authored a dozen books on this topic alone. One of his early works, *Israel's Final Holocaust,* became a national bestseller, and remains a popular book today. His in-depth study of the last Book of the Bible, *Revelation Revealed, Verse by Verse,* is considered by many to be the definitive study on the subject and is regarded as a classic.

Dr. Van Impe's interest in his books, as might be expected, is the influence they have in helping people understand the Word of God and make decisions for Christ. "The important thing is to answer people's questions and lead them to a closer relationship with God," he says. "That's why I wrote them. That's why we keep printing them. That's why we've given untold thousands of them away, particularly in overseas missions fields."

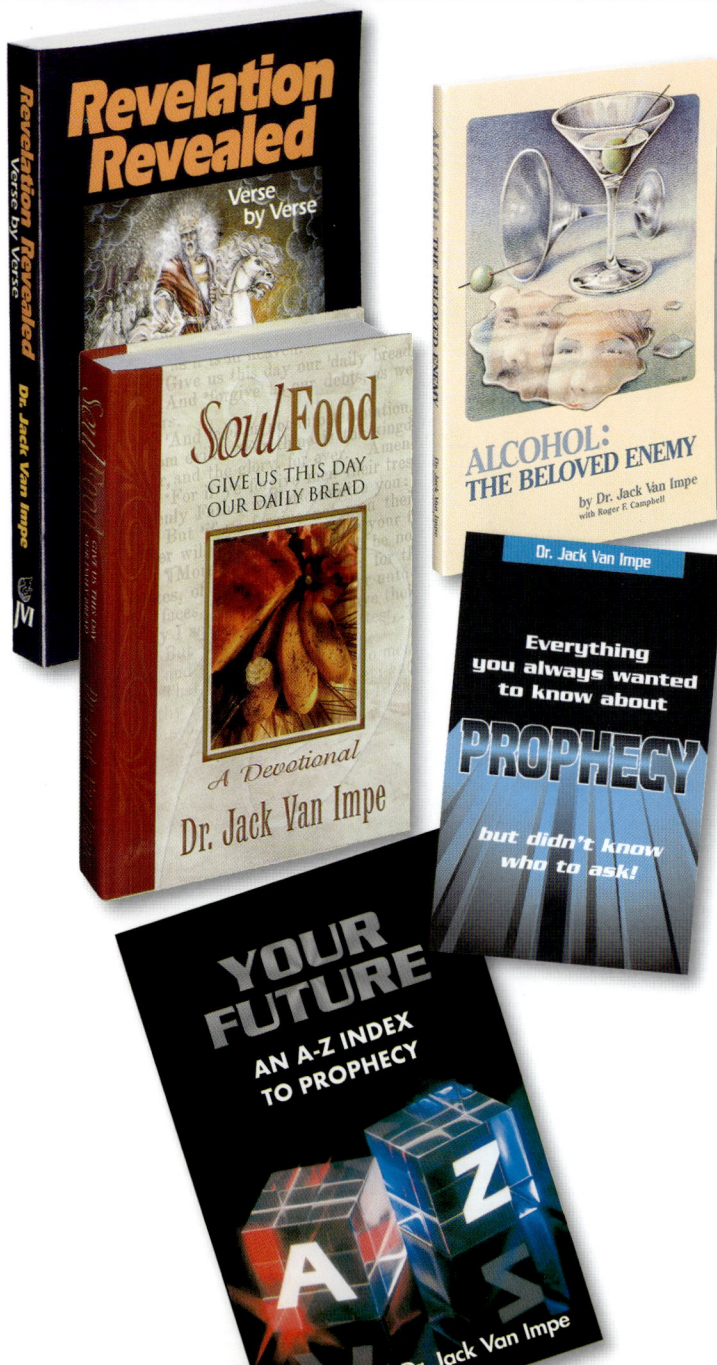

...In A Book —Jeremiah 30:2

Rexella Van Impe is also a popular author whose inspirational articles in *Perhaps Today* Magazine draw much comment and are reproduced (by permission) by several other Christian publications. Her commentaries also attract a heavy volume of "hits" on the ministry's Internet site.

Mrs. Van Impe has written numerous books, including: *The Tender Touch, Satisfied, Hope and Fear Not, Beware: Children in Peril, Is God Magic?, Mirror, Mirror, Who Am I Fooling?, Encounters, A Taste of Life, Reflections, Inside Out.*

Letters We Love...
about the book ministry

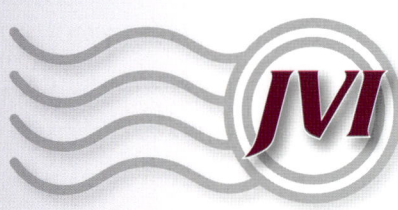

YOUR BOOKS ARE THE BEST

Out of all the books that I have on the Bible, your books are the best. I can follow and understand them. Your book on Revelation is beautiful!

—Rev. O.L., Los Angeles, California

JESUS IS LORD

You sure did surprise me with your book, *The Spirit of Antichrist*. I wasn't expecting to get anything free. Most ministries just ask, but you give. Because of your book I now know that Jesus is the Lord God Almighty—not just a mere created man.

—R.E.C., Vinton, California

11:59 AND COUNTING! TOTALLY AWESOME

My wife and I were saved just months ago. We just received the book *11:59...and Counting!* and read it in just four days—could not put it down! It is totally awesome. We're praying for you and are out spreading the Word.

—E. & S.B., York, Pennsylvania

BOOK BRINGS SOUL TO CHRIST

I listen to a local Christian talk show on radio. Yesterday a young man called in and said he had been in the cults, the occult, Tarot card reading, séances, etc. His girlfriend had given him a copy of your book, *Exorcism and the Spirit World*. He said, "I read it and it changed me. I want to come to Christ and get out of all that other stuff." The show host prayed with him and the young man asked Jesus to come into his heart and save him. Praise God for your book, Dr. Van Impe. It saved one more soul.

—M.K., San Bernardino, California

I AM NOW A NEW CREATURE

I am particularly grateful for the book, *The Tender Touch*. It was written just for me! There is a great change in my life and I am now a new creature. Rexella, I understand and appreciate the work the Lord has put in your hands in conjunction with your husband's ministry. My husband is a pastor in a remote village where we live with our three children. We appreciate the books by both of you for they improve our Bible knowledge.

—P.E., Nigeria

WISDOM FOUND IN VAN IMPE BOOKS

I have read many of your books and because of it I have become a different person. People notice the change in me and I find myself telling them what I have learned. What wisdom is hidden in your books!

—G.N., Cameroon

Letters We Love...
about the book ministry

VICTORY OVER DRINK

I recently read your book, *Sin's Explosion.* Thank you for the time and research that went into producing this masterpiece. It should be in the hands of every pastor and evangelist in the country. About five years ago I witnessed to a friend who was such a drunk he couldn't even hold a job. I gave him your book, *Alcohol, the Beloved Enemy.* The last I heard, he has victory over drink! Praise the Lord.
—W.B.M., Woodstock, Georgia

THIRTY PEOPLE COME TO THE LORD

I am a fellow minister and a supporter of your work. At a recent business seminar I was involved in, I used your book, *First Steps in a New Direction,* and 30 people made decisions for the Lord. Thank God for using your literature to bring the lost to Christ.
—T.S., Tualatin, Oregon

JVI BOOKS ARE FANTASTIC

A brother told me about your radio program and gave me some of your books to read. I went through them all, and everything inside was clear and understandable. In fact, it was fantastic! Thank you for your ministry.
—M.M., Panama

I Was In Prison, and Ye Came To Me   –Matthew 25:36

One of the most alarming problems in America is crime… and criminals… and the imprisoned. The United States leads the world in every category of violent crime and has the largest incarcerated population. In fact, overcrowded conditions are a major problem in jails, juvenile institutions, and state and federal prisons.

Nor is locking criminals up solving the problem. Conventional "corrections" agencies aren't having much success in rehabilitating society's offenders. The recidivism rate reaches as high as 85 percent—which means 85 of every 100 prisoners released will end up back in prison!

The only hope of reducing crime and lessening the need for prisons is by reaching out to prisoners in love and teaching them the Word of God while they are "inside." Dr. Jack Van Impe has been sensitive—and responsive—to this need for many years.

In response to the thousands of U.S. inmates who have written to the ministry after hearing or seeing a Van Impe program on radio or television, the ministry has provided tracts, books, Bibles, tapes, videos, Bible memorization cards, and gospel study aids. Thousands of prisoners have been enrolled in Bible study courses, and others have received counseling and encouragement by mail.

Overseas, the ministry has also provided large quantities of books, literature, Bibles, cassettes, videos, and other study materials to help local ministries minister to the spiritual needs of those in prison.

Today the ministry supports the work of various organizations specializing in prison ministry, and often refers inquiries from inmates to them. Great things are being accomplished in the lives of thousands of prisoners through the power of prayer and the Word of God.

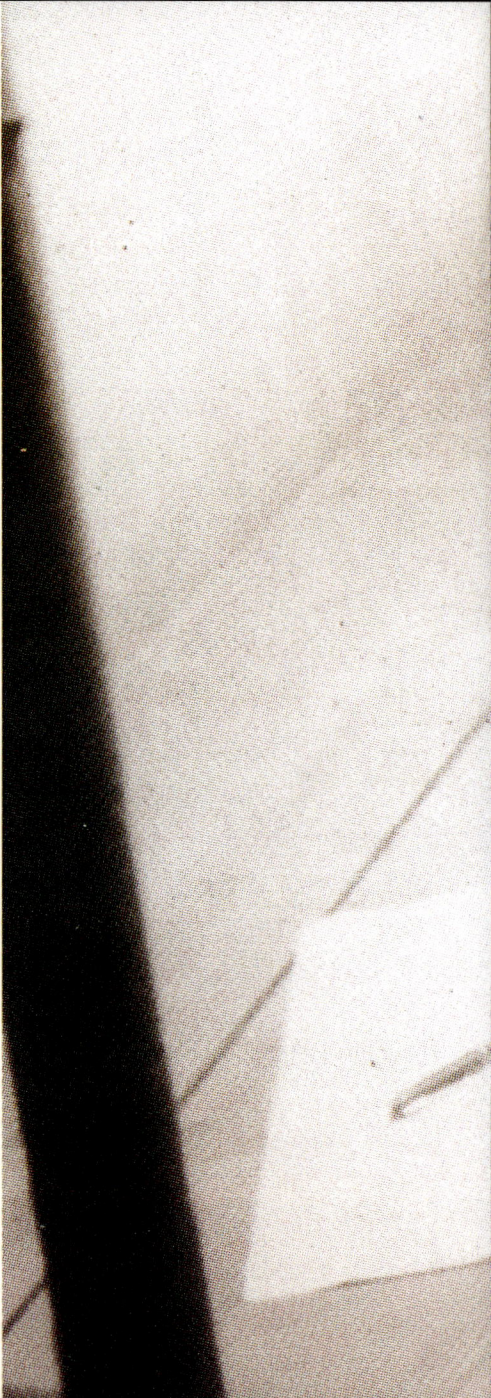

Letters We Love...
about the prison ministry

DEATH ROW INMATE SAVED

I am in prison but I'm no longer alone in my small death row cell. Thanks to you, I now share it with a friend named Jesus. I saw your TV program on TBN and your message got through to me. I'd heard the message of Jesus many times, but repeatedly postponed confessing my sin and giving my life to Him. You made me realize the meaning of the phrase, "now is the time of salvation." I am so grateful to you that I changed my life before it was too late. Thanks to your program I am no longer bound for hell.

—J.D.B

GOD'S LOVE REACHES PRISONER

Before I enrolled in your biblical studies, I was just wasting my life away here in prison. I wanted to turn to God and ask for help, but my bitterness would not let me. Through the Bible studies, I have been brought to God and an understanding of His love for me. Thanks.

—K.W., Montgomery, Pennsylvania

SAVED READING JVI LETTER

I became a Christian just a few days ago when I got a letter from Jack Van Impe Ministries. As I read, I decided to pray the sinner's prayer. A peace came over me which I cannot explain, but even here in prison I know that I am free. I cried, but my tears were for joy and release of sin.

—D.L., Maple, North Carolina

NEVER GOING BACK TO OLD LIFE

Thank you for caring so much for a useless convict like me. I have shot dope for a long time and it has burned my mind out. But, thank Jesus, I am alive even though in prison. The world needs more people like you and your ministry. Thanks to your message, I've seen the real me and turned to God. You helped me be saved from eternal hell. I will never go back to the life I was leading.

—J.P., Jackson, North Carolina

STUDIES BIBLE BY TAPE

I received the wonderful tapes you sent me. They are great. Since I can't read, the tapes help me so much. I've always wanted to read the Bible, and now I can study it by listening to your tapes.

—R.W., Knoxville, Tennessee

Letters We Love...
about the prison ministry

MURDERER ACCEPTS CHRIST

I am an inmate in the Drumheller Institution doing 10 years for killing my friend in a fight. I watched your TV show and your message got to me. I know what I did is wrong and I asked God to forgive me and Jesus to come into my life.

—J.H., Drumheller, Alberta, Canada

PROGRAM WAS TURNING POINT

I am presently serving a prison sentence of 34-68 years. I am only 21 years of age. I have allowed Satan to rule my life too long. I have been wandering around as a blind and lost sinner. I have cursed God and rebuked His Word until Friday night when I watched your program and received Jesus.

—J.F.

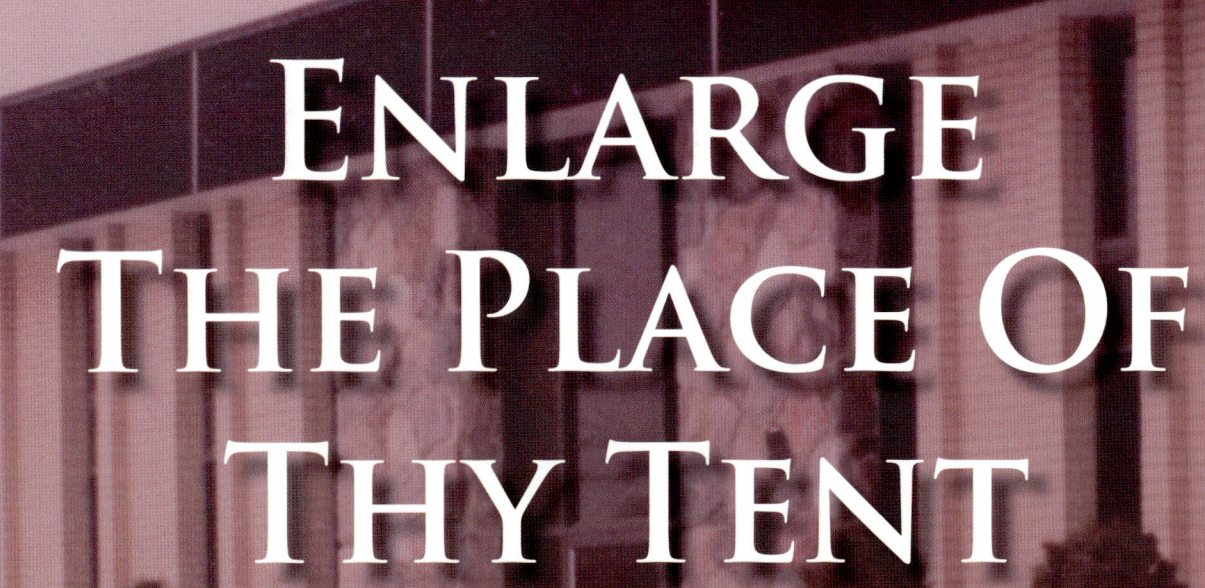

Jack Van Impe Ministries International World Outreach Center

In 1989, Jack Van Impe Ministries moved to a new, permanent headquarters building. Custom designed for the ministry's needs, the new center provided expanded office and warehouse space for the organization's rapid growth. Also, a functional television production center, with a sound stage, control room, audio booth, and edit suite, with state-of-the-art cameras and equipment, were included. The facility also has its own satellite uplink dish.

By bringing all ministry functions from four locations under one roof, and eliminating costly studio rental, the new World Outreach Center dramatically improved efficiency and actually helped curtail rising costs. The building's functional design and simple, tasteful furnishings reflect the Van Impe's emphasis on excellence, value, and modesty.

We Are Labourers Together With God –I Corinthians 3:9

Jack Van Impe Ministries is staffed by dedicated people who regard their work as a ministry calling rather than simply a career. Many who work in the World Outreach Center measure their tenure in decades, and have been part of the development and growth of the ministry from a small crusade team to an international multi-media organization with wide-ranging evangelistic outreaches. Dr. and Mrs. Van Impe meet often with the staff for chapel services.

Dr. Charles (Chuck) Ohman is Vice President of Jack Van Impe Ministries and the golden-toned announcer on the weekly telecast and video productions. A longtime friend of the Van Impes, he joined their areawide crusade team to organize and direct the mass choirs and lead singing in the services. A renowned trumpet player, he has recorded and made numerous appearances with his own group, a talented brass ensemble.

Mr. Ken Vancil is Executive Director for the ministry, overseeing all the day-to-day operations of the organization. Mr. Vancil came up through the ranks, starting in the warehouse, then heading the mail counseling and prison ministry operations before moving to the top management spot.

Long term department heads have a combined total of over 150 years of experience at Jack Van Impe Ministries. Willa Derenge works in the Finance and Donor Services departments; Emmajean Spach oversees the Data Entry department; and Rev. Reuben Ellis directs the Ministry Services department. June Hazen has faithfully served as the Van Impe's Administrative Secretary. Jim Taylor's photographic skill and versatility in sound, lighting, and electronics have made him invaluable over the years.

State-of-the-art computer system enables ministry personnel to process a large flow of mail, maintain donor records, handle requests for ministry materials, and prepare mailing labels for newsletters and publications.

Warehouse and order fulfillment areas utilize every inch of available space to stock adequate supplies of hundreds of titles of books, cassettes, videos, publications, and other ministry items to facilitate fast handling of product orders.

Chapel service is a highlight for the Jack Van Impe Ministries employees who gather to pray for the organization's donors and friends. Dr. and Mrs. Van Impe often attend to speak and pray with staff members.

New Television Format:
Jack Van Impe Presents

Interpreting Today's News In The Light of Bible Prophecy

The launching of a totally new weekly television program in 1988 marked the culmination of a startling, staggering series of developments that reinvented Jack Van Impe Ministries.

Dr. and Mrs. Van Impe remained the same dedicated, dynamic ministry team they had always been.

Their message, mission, and purpose stayed the same.

Virtually everything else was refined, improved, streamlined, and re-designed for maximum efficiency, economy, and effectiveness.

The ministry moved into a beautiful new World Outreach Center, which combined under one roof the occupants and contents of two separate office buildings, a warehouse, and a storage building.

Even more significant, in the heart of the new headquarters was a state-of-the-art television sound stage, with adjoining control rooms, sound booth, and production center. The new studio was equipped with new cameras, videotape equipment, effects generators, mixers, control boards—everything a top quality production studio or network TV station would have installed…including a brand-new satellite uplink dish installed on the roof of the building.

By having its own studio and equipment in-house, the ministry saved hundreds of thousands of dollars in rental costs annually and kept the Van Impes and the TV production staff from traveling miles through congested traffic into dark and dangerous areas each time they taped the telecast.

THE FASTEST HALF-HOUR ON TELEVISION

Not only did the television ministry have an efficient, economical new production facility, *it had a new program!* No longer did the Van Impe program look like a variety show, an entertainment "special," a documentary, or include preaching segments from crusades or public meetings.

Jack Van Impe Presents was a totally new format, featuring Rexella and Jack at a network news desk. The new telecast emphasized Bible prophecy from beginning to end. Rexella read up-to-the-minute news reports, showcased headlines, photos, cartoons, and video clips of major current events. Then she asked her husband for his commentary on each issue.

With 15,000 Bible verses memorized and catalogued by topic in his mind, Dr. Van Impe analyzed and explained each report, quoting in machine gun fashion the relevant and applicable prophetic scriptures.

Then Rexella would present the next topic. Back and forth, smoothly and rapidly, the Van Impes examined all the news developments of the week in the light of Bible prophecy. So intriguing and fascinating was the fast-moving tableau that the program's half hour flew by. Viewers were often incredulous that the time was used up so quickly.

Each program ended with Dr. Van Impe's summation of the prophetic impact of the week's impact and an emphasis on the overwhelming importance of each viewer making sure of his or her personal salvation. Then he led a simple, no-hype sinner's prayer.

The program was immediately dubbed "the fastest half hour on TV!"

The popularity and success of the telecast was immediate and overwhelming. The program reached people who wanted to hear about the Bible as well as the unchurched. In fact, because of the news format and the prime time airings, many viewers didn't realize at first that they were watching a religious presentation. It was apparent the format reached far more unchurched people than typical church and pulpit formats.

People began calling and writing to express their interest and approval. They said *Jack Van Impe Presents* was the most informative program they'd ever watched…the most exciting…the most thought provoking. They were intrigued by the high energy and warm rapport of the husband-wife team. They felt Van Impe was the best-read person they'd ever heard, and were amazed at his correlation of world news and Bible prophecy…at his rapid fire quoting of verse after verse.

Then they came back to watch a second time, and a third. That says a lot. People who never watched another religious program—especially people of other religions, such as Jews, Hindus, Muslims—told the Van Impes they wouldn't miss a week.

KEYS TO SUCCESS

What made the new program so effective? Dr. Van Impe gives credit to Rexella's warmth and sensitivity. "People sense that we are completely comfortable working together. Rexella presents just enough of the current issues and news events to set the stage for my commentary and teaching from the Bible. She knows my mind so well that she always knows just what should come next!"

Rexella notes that the news format is possible only because of her husband's years of intense study and preparation. "No one could possibly memorize in a few days the hundreds of applicable Bible verses for the various topics discussed on our weekly telecast. But Jack is able to draw them from the vast storehouse he has accumulated from a lifetime of disciplined study. Besides being so impressively knowledgeable, he is so excited and dynamic—his enthusiasm is irresistible.

Jack Van Impe Presents is carried on hundreds of broadcast stations and on multiplied thousands of cable hook-ups to major nationwide networks—including WGN, VISION, ACTS, INSP, Cornerstone TV, and TBN. The program reaches some 25,000 cities and towns in North America alone. The telecast is also carried on the TBN South African stations, in Puerto Rico and American Samoa, and aired via satellite on Christian Channel Europe. We are now in 211 nations weekly.

Through this enormous weekly coverage, Dr. and Mrs. Van Impe easily reach more people in a single half hour than they did in years of crusades. Precious souls from 160 nations have responded to the Van Impe's presentation of the message of God's love.

The quality of the program's content and production values attracted the attention of the respected Religion in Media organization, which presented Jack Van Impe Ministries with its prestigious "Angel" award for excellence in media presentation. The "Angel" is equivalent to the secular television industry's "Emmy" award. Over the years, Van Impe productions have received 33 "Angel" awards, and both Jack and Rexella have been honored with "Golden Angel" awards for lifetime achievement.

Letters We Love...
about the weekly telecast

PROGRAM STANDS OUT FROM THE REST

My wife and I watch your wonderful program every week. There is a wide variety of religious programs but yours stands out from the rest. It motivates us to learn more about the subjects you present. Mrs. Van Impe makes the program even more enjoyable with her down-to-earth, loving sincerity. We pray for you and look forward to meeting you in heaven.

—B. & J.J., Ocean Bluff, Maine

GREETINGS FROM CHINA!

Through the miracle of satellites, I have just seen your TV broadcast here in Peking, China. Please send me some of your booklets.

—G.C.A., Peking, China

DYING HUSBAND ACCEPTS CHRIST THROUGH TELECAST

I lost my husband to lung cancer, but before he died he accepted the Lord. Most of the credit goes to you and Rexella. We never missed your program on TV. I praise the Lord for both of you and the wonderful message of Christ you brought us from week to week.

—Mrs. L.M., Nashville, Tennessee

KEEP ON KEEPING ON

How I appreciate your work for the Lord. I'm impressed by your dedication first to the Lord and then to each other. It's refreshing to see a husband and wife ministry that shows no competitiveness, resentment, or animosity. I personally consider your ministry one of the best. Keep on keeping on.

—L.R.W., Meadville, Pennsylvania

AN INTERNATIONAL MISSION

I pray God will strengthen you in your work to bring the gospel to all nations. I am from Iran and my wife is from Vietnam. I am an ex-Moslem and she is an ex-Buddhist. We are parents of four children who are wonderful gifts from God to us. We love and consider you part of our family. Our week is not complete if we don't get to see your TV program. I am also a student of Bible prophecy and am studying to help bring Jewish people to Yeshua (Jesus). We attend a Messianic congregation. When I hear your program it is like my own heart speaking through your voice. Thank God for you and Rexella.

—D.R., Anaheim, California

Letters We Love...
about the weekly telecast

VIPs ARE WATCHING

Did you know that some congressmen have asked that your program be aired on week nights in our area so they can view? Please stay on the air to get your message to them. Important people are watching you. Praise the Lord.

—R.L.S., Arlington, Virginia

TBN VIEWER

Your program blesses my heart and spirit. I love to hear of the Bible prophecies and am impressed by your great knowledge of the Word of God. I watch your program on TBN.

—H., West Indies

FEELS CLEARER ABOUT WORLD

How I enjoy watching your show—I always feel clearer about what is happening in the world today after the program. I admire your knowledge of the Bible and appreciate your including the salvation prayer at the show's close. Thanks for being there to show me the way.

—K.C., Santa Monica, California

ACCURATE AND DEPENDABLE

Thank you for helping people all over the world to see that we are in the last days and to reorient our lives toward God. Your show has been a great blessing in my life. I am absolutely convinced that your interpretation of sacred scripture is accurate and dependable. I'm delighted you do not attack Catholics, and appreciate your use of statements from the current and past popes to reinforce the other sources of information you use.

—M.G., Austin, Texas

TV MY COMPANION

I am 70 years old and TV is my main "companion" since my husband passed away. I watch your show every Wednesday—it is just beautiful. You get right to the point and I sit spellbound—I don't want to even answer the phone for fear of missing something.

a—I.J., Hammond, Louisiana

PROGRAM COMES IN LOUD AND CLEAR

I live in the Dominican Republic and receive your program on TBN's satellite. You come in loud and clear. I'm sure many broadcasters don't realize they are being received by thousands of dishes throughout the Caribbean, Central and South American areas.

—B.F., Dominican Republic

KEEP UP THE GOOD WORK

It's so encouraging to see a husband and wife team like yours operating in the wisdom, love, and power of God. It inspires me to have greater trust in Jesus' love. Truly the Holy Spirit is being poured out on all flesh.

—L.B., Hawthorne, California

FULL OF GOD'S LOVE

Thank God for your TV program. You both have such love for people. Your smiles warm our hearts, and your tears show that you feel like we do. You are "real" and full of the love of God and the Holy spirit.

—P.F., Knoxville, Tennessee

Letters We Love...
about the weekly telecast

YOU'RE MY PASTOR

You have been my pastor for the last six months. I have been ill and unable to go to church. Your program means so much to me and I know it is helping others. I am praying for your work. God bless you.

—P.R., St,. Albans, West Virginia

STRENGTHENED BY TEACHING

I was watching your program and received such a tremendous blessing! I had been battling depression, but after hearing only a few moments of your anointed message—WOW! My spirit became so excited and I felt such a strength from hearing you teach. I praise God that He has given you so much wisdom and understanding in His Word!

—M.S., Fort Walton Beach, Florida

Letters We Love...
about the weekly telecast

NO NONSENSE MESSAGE

It is a real joy and encouragement to watch your weekly TV program. Your no-nonsense approach to soulwinning based on scriptural facts and prophecy is refreshing. To turn on the TV and hear you teach straight from the Word of God is truly a blessing.

—R.L., Ashland, Ohio

SAVED FROM SATANISM

I was flipping through the channels one evening, and it just seemed that God made me stop at your program. I had started to get into Satanism, but your program was really like a slap in the face. Now I have a greater love in me than ever before. God filled the empty space that Satan said he could fill. Now I'm on that narrow road to heaven instead of that 8-lane highway to hell. Thank you for your program—I enjoy it every week.

—M.C., Penrose, Colorado

BLESSING TO MILLIONS

My wife and I truly enjoy your program. We hear God's Word come alive! You explain the Scriptures in such a way that we can't wait for your next program. Jack and Rexella, you are a blessing to millions! My friends and I discuss your programs with excitement.

—F.S., Orleans, Ontario, Canada

WITNESS

I love your program. Every time I get the least bit complacent, there will be something on your program that makes me start witnessing again. I know Jesus is coming back soon. Keep up the good work.

—J.F.M., Salt Lake City, Utah

> *To date, tens of thousands have repeated the prayer for salvation at the conclusion of the telecast.*

VIDEO EVANGELISM

Sharing The Truth of God's Word
In The Homes of Spiritually Hungry People

Undoubtedly, one of the most powerful and far-reaching outreaches of the ministry is the use of videocassettes loaded with a dynamic gospel presentation for use by individuals at home. To date, Dr. and Mrs. Van Impe have produced one hundred fifty different video titles and distributed millions of copies.

Industry experts have determined that an average video is watched by some 20 viewers. This means that the Van Impe video ministry alone has probably touched the lives of up to 25 million people!

The videos include some of the Van Impe's nationwide prime time television specials, special multi-volume productions of classic Van Impe works like *Revelation Revealed,* and timely prophetic teachings like *Startling Revelations: Pope John Paul II; 2001—Countdown to the Millennium;* and *Daniel, Final End Time Mysteries Unsealed.*

In addition to the wide circulation of the videos via TV marketing across North America, the ministry has donated multiplied thousands of videos to mission agencies that have placed them in the hands of national ministers in scores of countries on virtually every continent. As always, Dr. Van Impe's "bottom line" interest in this outreach is *souls*—winning people for Christ.

Letters We Love...
about the video ministry

VIDEO INTRODUCED ME TO CHRISTIANITY

I recently visited my aunt in Florida. She is a Christian and had your video, "Russia, World III, and Armageddon." I watched it with great interest—it was my first introduction to Christianity, salvation, and life hereafter. I said the salvation prayer with you and gave my life to Jesus. I was baptized in water before I left Florida.

—M.M., Sunnyside, New York

CAN'T GET SAVED FOR CHILDREN

We enjoy your television program each week and also your videos. We ordered *The Great Escape* and our daughter was so touched by it that she gave her heart to the Lord. We are regular church members but you can't get saved for your children. You can only pray for them. Thanks for your ministry—keep up the good work.

—A.E., Marion, Indiana

JVI VIDEOS GO LIKE HOTCAKES

I'm so grateful for your contribution of videos here in the Philippines. We're having good results with them. Your videos are so popular—they go just like hotcakes. Everybody wants to borrow them and show them in their homes and to their friends. Young people are attracted to "The Occult World" and "The Great Escape." They are hungry to know more about the Rapture. Your tapes are powerful and are making a difference in the lives of our people. Thank you for blessing us.

—J.G.S., Philippines

REDEDICATED LIFE TO CHRIST

After ordering and viewing your video, A.D. 2000—The End?," I rededicated my life to Christ. Since then, my wife and 11-year-old son also have gotten saved. God bless you for your television and video ministry.

—D.W., Wheelersburg, Ohio

VIDEO IS WITNESSING TOOL

We were very inspired by the enormous biblical truths in your video. You and Mrs. Van Impe are God-sent to this dying world. After viewing the tape, we decided to have a cook-out and family reunion for 35 people. We showed your video at this gathering and, as a result, two were saved and two rededicated their lives to Jesus Christ. All four are living godly lives today and are witnessing to others.

—K. & R.R., Chesapeake, Virginia

SOMETHING WONDERFUL HAPPENED

We recently ordered the *Revelation Revealed* video set and the "Heaven" video. We were very pleased with them. But when we showed them to my husband's parents, something wonderful happened! My husband's mother accepted Christ at the end. God bless you and your work.

—D. and E.Z., Eagan, Minnesota

Letters We Love...
about the video ministry

EIGHT SAVED THROUGH VIDEO SET

I ordered the *Revelation Revealed* video set and, after viewing them, sent them to the church where a friend of mine attends. She said the tapes were shown in church services…and eight people were saved as a result!

—Mrs. A.B., Lawton, Oklahoma

VIDEO PARTY

Recently my wife and I invited several of our family and friends over to our house for a video party. Everyone enjoyed your strong prophetic message and it sparked a great discussion. There is much to ponder and prepare for. I plan on sharing the video with my entire family.

—S.B., Joplin, Missouri

VIDEOS FOR FRIENDS

My husband and I are ordering 10 copies of your videocassette, "The 90s, Startling End-time Signs, and Your Future." We are so excited about this message that we want to share it with our friends in various areas.

—L.V., Indianapolis, Indiana

MAKING THE ROUNDS

A few weeks ago we received "America in Prophecy" and another of your videos. God is really using these tapes. My husband works at a paper mill and after telling his co-workers about the tapes, they wanted to see them, too. So they're borrowing them for the weekends. It's amazing how the Lord is using these videos to reach the lost. Only God knows how much will be accomplished for His glory.

—P. & D.K., Franklin, Ohio

VIDEO HELPS WIN ENTIRE FAMILY

Several months ago my husband's parents sent us your video, "Russia, World War III, and Armageddon." After watching it that evening, my husband and I and our three children all accepted the Lord and were born again! Now we've been ordering your videos ourselves. After studying them, we pass them on to others.

—Mr. and Mrs. C.H., Prince George, B.C., Canada

The Jack Van Impe Ministries International "home page" continually strives not only to be the most comprehensive and up-to-date Bible prophecy website on the Internet but also a daily wellspring of inspiration for believers and help for seekers. It includes a listing of ministry outreaches, along with a statement of faith and the organization's mission statement.

Complementing the evangelistic ministries of Dr. Van Impe, the site features Real Video and audio streaming of the ministry's weekly telecast, and a daily news update. There is a frequently updated personal message from Dr. Van Impe, and a weekly "Tender Touch" article from Rexella.

The website has been tremendously popular, averaging tens of thousands of "hits" a day. Videostreaming of the weekly telecast served 250,000 viewers in the first month alone.

Site visitors may also access a Scripture Memorization Program, full-text books on Bible prophecy, the international television schedule, plus a ministry product catalog section, and a guest book.

Recipient of the "Best of the Christian Web" award for 1997, the Van Impe cyberlink is a tremendous new outreach for the gospel.

Letters We Love...
from our internet site

BEEN ON 3 HOURS—BE BACK TOMORROW

I read your *"Everything You Always Wanted To Know About Prophecy."* It was great information—I couldn't stop till I read it all. This is very good stuff. You wrote it where I could follow most things in the Bible. I have been on your page for over 3 hours. I will come back tomorrow and check some of the other things you have here. Thank you.

—*W.H., Internet Guest Book*

LOOK FORWARD TO "INTELLIGENCE BRIEFING"

I look forward to your *"Intelligence Briefing"* every month. I pass the information along to my pastor and he too enjoys! He has even incorporated the information into sermons. Thank you so much for your service to God.

—*P.T., Internet Guest Book*

EXCITING STUFF!

I am thoroughly thankful to our heavenly Father for sending the both of you to this world as leaders and believers. I watch your weekly program—haven't missed one in over two months. Exciting stuff!!!! I just ordered the Rapture video and look forward to receiving and viewing it. Thanks again for your ministry and may God continue to bless you.

—*M.C., Internet Guest Book*

DOING GREAT JOB

Does the sun ever set on a JVI program, transmission, and/or broadcast? You are doing a great job of disseminating various elements of God's Word throughout the world.

—*T.C., Internet Guest Book*

BLESSING TO WATCH

You two are a blessing to watch. I'm excited to see your ministry expanding more and more. The whole globe needs to see and hear the truth.

—*T.S., Internet Guest Book*

THIS IS WONDERFUL

I think your home page is wonderful. I have learned so much from this and also from your videos and books. Keep up the good work.

—*L.W., Internet Guest Book*

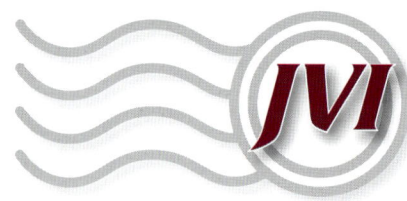

Letters We Love...
from our internet site

Oscar & Louise Van Impe

For I was my father's son, tender and only beloved in the sight of my mother.
—Proverbs 4:3

Oscar and Louise Van Impe left their home in Flanders, Belgium, in October 1929, just two weeks after their wedding day. They planned to come to America and work until they had saved enough to make a good start in life.

It was a good plan, but they arrived in the United States at the time the land of promise became the land of problems—at about the time of the stock market crash that brought the Great Depression. So instead of making their fortune, they worked in the pickle factory, the sugar beet and vegetable fields, and finally in the Plymouth automobile factory in Detroit—at 63 cents an hour.

To augment their income, Oscar and Louise began to frequent the taverns and nightclubs in Detroit's Belgian sector where Oscar entertained playing the accordion. When their son, Jack, was born, he was taken on the nightclub circuit with them, and was taught to play the accordion by age 5.

Oscar's discipline, drive, and desire to excel left an indelible mark on his son. By both advice and example, this industrious father succeeded in teaching his son the importance of giving himself completely to any task, instilling a love for hard work.

The quiet and tender nature of Louise also shows through. Her keen sense of humor and love of life, along with a sweet sense of trust and faith, provided a wholesome balance in their family life.

Shortly after their conversion several years later, the couple felt a call to return to Belgium to share the gospel with their unsaved families in the old country. They had to leave their son, Jack, alone in America where he was attending Bible College. This must have been a great act of faith for them.

When they returned to the U.S. a few years later, the Van Impes were among the most faithful supporters of the growing international outreach of their son's ministry. For the rest of his life, Oscar spent up to five hours a day praying, interceding for the partners of the ministry, beseeching God to bless the ministry and all who labored in it, and seeking the Lord for every other prayer request he knew about.

Oscar's daily prayer vigil was important to him. Once when invited to take a trip to the Holy Land, he graciously declined the offer. "No, I really can't go," he said. "The travel and sightseeing would take too much time away from my prayer schedule. I've got to stick with my prayer life. Besides, I'll get to see the Holy Land when I return with Jesus and all His saints to Jerusalem."

Surely the tremendous accomplishments of Jack Van Impe Ministries are part of the spiritual legacy of Oscar and Louise Van Impe, now both a part of the "great cloud of witnesses" in heaven described in Hebrews 12.

Rex & Esther Shelton

By Rexella Van Impe

> *Thy father and thy mother shall be glad, and she that bare thee shall rejoice.*
> —Proverbs 23:35

My brothers and I were blessed to be born to some of the best parents in the whole world. The Christian example and training we received at their hands helped prepare each of us to accept Christ as Saviour at an early age, and no doubt, was influential in our choice of Christian service careers.

We grew up in church. Our week's activities, our social events revolved around the church. My older brother, Bob, and I sang together for the Lord from the time we were children. In my earliest memories, serving God was the expected and "normal" path for our whole family.

My father didn't send me and my brothers, Bob and Don, to church with my mother—he took us to church as a family. When I'd get up to sing my "specials," Dad was always there, his face shining with approval and oftentimes with tears running down his face. In later years, when Jack and I were young evangelists, whenever we were within fifty or a hundred miles, Dad and Mother would drive over to be in our services. That meant he'd only get four or five hours sleep because he was up each morning at 5:30 a.m. for work.

My dad was a quality control inspector on a General Motors auto assembly line. I'll never forget when he took me to see his work. I was so proud of him—I thought he was the most important person in that plant, and it made me look up to him even more.

I knew my father. He was a real, flesh and blood, down-to-earth person. He was not afraid to share his struggles and troubles openly— not to burden his children but to let us see how he worked through hard times and faced adversity…and how he trusted God. He openly showed us the reality of trusting his Heavenly Father.

My dad taught me how to live. And he also taught me how to die.

When his life came to an end, the whole family gathered in his hospital room to spend the last precious hours with him. He suffered in dignity…and died in peace.

Shortly before he crossed over into heaven, I was alone with him a few minutes. I asked, "Dad, we don't have a lot of time left together in this world. Is there anything you have to tell me?" After a long moment of silence, he squeezed my hand gently and said, "Fulfill the reason for which you've been born!" Those words have been my goal ever since—to give my best to the work of God that is my life's calling.

PRECIOUS MEMORIES

I remember my mother with complete admiration and respect. So much of *who* I am and *what* I am is a result of her loving guidance and positive influence. I first learned love at Mother's knee through her touch and her care.

It was from Mother's voice that I first heard music, which has been

such an important part of my whole life and ministry. In fact, I remember hearing music before I remember uttering words as a baby. I have no doubt that my love for singing came from her.

Humility was a quality Mother taught me by example. To this day she has the most beautiful, unassuming spirit of anyone I know. To me she is a perfectly blended combination of the biblical sisters, Mary and Martha. She always spent time worshiping the Lord. I've walked into her bedroom many times and found her on her knees or reading her Bible. But her personal devotions were always balanced with practical service to others.

From Mother I learned the secret of inner beauty—of filling my heart and mind with love and wholesomeness and letting them permeate my entire being. There are so many other qualities she taught me—tenderness, a sense of duty, a living expression of the gifts of the Holy Spirit.

But I must mention one more—I learned wisdom through my mother. Wisdom comes from the Lord, according to the Book of Proverbs. But Mother certainly was a *living symbol* of that divinely-given quality. She always had the answers to my questions, always knew the right thing to do in every situation, always seemed to know when to act and when to wait.

Last but not least—Mother has always been extremely popular at the Van Impe house for another special reason. For years she has proclaimed to everybody that she has the finest son-in-law in all the world!

Mom went home to be with the Lord in 2003.

What Others Say

Comments By Friends and Fellow-Laborers

Be Thou An Example of the Believers...

Dear Dr. Van Impe,

I had the joy and honor of traveling with you across our nation for four years, conducting over 450 banquets. Not once did I take for granted the opportunity I had of working so closely with "The Walking Bible." What a thrill it was to spend literally thousands of hours laughing, crying, praying, and rejoicing in the Lord with you.

While some other evangelists traveled in their own custom jets, you chose to save the Lord's money by riding with me in our work van. In fact, I still remember the times when Mrs. Van Impe was with us, which meant the only place left for you to sit in the two-seat van was in the middle of the cargo boxes. Many of these trips required traveling 250-300 miles a day.

What really impressed my friends when I told them about you folks was that besides not having a real seat, you spent those many uncomfortable hours studying and memorizing scripture. Still more people were shocked to hear that you got out and pumped gasoline when we stopped to fill up at service stations.

I want you to know that I love and appreciate you. In a day of extravagance and waste, I do not know of anybody who is a better steward of God's money than you. Every step of the way you are conscientious and aware of how it's being used.

Jack Van Impe Ministries was not born overnight but started with two young servants eager to serve the Lord with all their might. I cannot begin to imagine the sacrifices you made in the early years, oftentimes not getting paid for weeks of meetings, all the while living out of a suitcase and even on occasion sleeping overnight in your car.

Thank God that after all these years you are still sensitive and concerned with the money God's people sacrificially give in support of your ministry. I'm so thankful that I can have a part in this wonderful ministry that ministers to tens of thousands of Christians and reaches the lost for Christ. You can count on my continued support. I only wish I could do more.

    Your friend,

    Byron Lewis

Why We Support Jack Van Impe Ministries

Dear Dr. Van Impe,

There are a couple of important reasons why my wife, Rose, and I, have chosen to support the work of Jack Van Impe Ministries.

First and foremost, this ministry helped saved me from the almost certain loss of my "passport" to heaven. I had known Jesus for many years when I detoured into cultism. The worst part is that I was taking my family with me.

I found cultism to be very fascinating—especially psychic healing. I met a cult preacher who could insert his fingers into a human body with without pain or blood. He would also go into trances and allow the spirits of dead people to take over and talk through him.

One night as I was twirling the TV dial, Jack Van Impe came on the screen…and I began to watch. His message brought to my remembrance all I had previously learned about God…and much more. This was during the time when the ministry was giving away tapes and literature by the wheelbarrow load! Well, it was not wasted—I was one of the beneficiaries of that generosity.

Brother Jack, when we meet in heaven you can be joyous in knowing that I am one of the fruits of your labor.

That was many years ago, and the rest is history. Today I have my "passport" in top shape and will never allow it to be put into jeopardy again. I realize the Holy Spirit led me to turn on the Van Impe telecast, but it could not have happened if Jack and Rexella had not dedicated themselves to the Lord's work.

The second reason I support this ministry is its policy of making the Lord's Word available to all who need it. This makes me realize the ministry needs and deserves some dedicated support. Each time I have money to put into the Lord's work, as I pray, I feel led to send most of it to Jack Van Impe Ministries. What a thrill to see all that God is doing all over the world through its outreaches.

    Your friend,

    Bob Madej

When that man is Dr. Jack Van Impe, he is accomplishing more than at any time in his life and enthusiastically looking forward to the future. "God has helped me memorize 15,000 Scripture verses and learn a great deal about the Bible and prophecy," he says. "I have more to share now than ever before. It would be a crime to even think of retiring. Besides, I love what I am doing—ministry is my life!"

Rexella agrees. "Jack will never retire…and that makes me happy. Because that means I'm not going to retire, either. We have a very young audience. TV statistics show that our strongest audience segments are from ages 18 to 45. So as long as God gives us health and strength—and I know He will—we'll keep going.

"Did you know that Dr. Van Impe has never missed a service because of illness in 58 years? Not a one! I remember times when he was so sick backstage that he looked positively green. I've seen him throw up in a trash can, then go out and preach. And I recall when he hurt his back and was so painful he could hardly walk. For a week or two he had to sit in a chair to preach, but he never missed a service."

Indeed, the Van Impes live to work. They have a modest, simple lifestyle and an orderly, amazingly-productive routine. Had they wished to acquire a fortune, quit working and take it easy, they easily could have been multi-millionaires years ago just from the royalties on their books, tapes, and videos. But all the earnings from their publications and productions have been given to the ministry from the beginning.

In fact, money is so *un*important to them that they have never sought a salary increase in their whole career. The nine-member board of directors of Jack Van Impe Ministries for the United States and Canada has initiated all their salary adjustments, sometimes over their protests.

And despite the tremendous success the Van Impes have seen in all their ministry ventures, ministering face to face to more than ten million people in public meetings, reaching multiplied millions more through global radio and television, and helping win at least a million souls or more to Christ, Jack and Rexella Van Impe have kept a personal identity with individuals.

Mrs. Van Impe is greeted by name when she slips into a favorite shop in the shopping mall near her home. Sometimes several of the sales clerks will come over to speak to her. She quietly uses such opportunities to share a simple word of witness. "I've had the opportunity to lead several of the sales girls to the Lord in the dressing room," she says. "It's such a joy to be able to win their trust and really be a friend to them. The other day a young lady at another store said to me, 'Mrs. Van Impe, you're the only customer who ever really looks at me, who sees me as a person.' My, what a great compliment that was to me."

Recently, driving home from a two week trip to Florida where Dr. Van Impe had spoken at a large prophecy conference, the couple stopped to eat at Burger King. Several people in the restaurant recognized them and came over to say, "We watch your TV program all the time."

After they'd gotten their food and finished eating, a young college student came over to the table. After a minute's conversation, he hesitantly mentioned that he had drifted away from the Lord, but had been watching the telecast. "You know, you've really touched my life," he said.

Dr. Van Impe smiled and said, "I'm glad we've touched you, but the important question is—Are you right with the Lord now?"

Dropping his head, the young man replied, "Well, I don't think so."

Reaching out and taking the boy's hand, Dr. Van Impe said, "Then this is the time. Do you want to accept Christ right here, right now?"

Tears streaming down his cheeks, the young man nodded and said, "Yes, Dr. Van Impe, yes I do." So they prayed together at the table in the corner of Burger King. And when they were finished, another soul had found the Lord.

This is a striking example of Dr. Jack Van Impe in action, dedicated, dynamic…a man and his mission.

DR. JACK VAN IMPE

Dynamic and Dedicated

A Man and His Mission

Jack Van Impe

Dr. Van Impe's ministry has brought more than 2 million souls to the foot of the cross seeking salvation. The renowned and respected Bible scholar and prophecy expert presently lays plans for the largest expansion his ministry has ever attempted.

In his crusades, conducted in ballparks and stadiums, ten million attended services in 1100 cities within 50 nations.

Presently, Jack and Rexella Van Impe reach millions weekly via global television and the Internet. Letters arrive annually from those whose lives have been touched in 211 nations through their weekly television shows, videos, books, and web site.

Dr. Van Impe has been recognized in seven national and international "Who's Who" books, has received 33 Angel Awards, and 17 Doctor's degrees.

After more than 50 years of ministry, Dr. Van Impe remains "Dynamic and Dedicated" and looks forward to even greater days because he is a man with a God-appointed mission.